CAMPAIGN 426

SIEGE OF KAZAN 1552

Ivan the Terrible Breaks the Kazan Khanate

MARK GALEOTTI ILLUSTRATED BY ANGEL GARCÍA PINTO

OSPREY PUBLISHING
Bloomsbury Publishing Plc
Kemp House, Chawley Park, Cumnor Hill, Oxford OX2 9PH, UK
Bloomsbury Publishing Ireland Limited,
29 Earlsfort Terrace, Dublin 2, D02 AY28, Ireland
Bloomsbury Publishing Inc.
1359 Broadway, 12th Floor, New York, NY 10018, USA
E-mail: info@ospreypublishing.com
www.ospreypublishing.com

OSPREY is a trademark of Osprey Publishing Ltd

First published in Great Britain in 2026

© Osprey Publishing Ltd, 2026

All rights reserved. No part of this publication may be: i) reproduced or transmitted in any form, electronic or mechanical, including photocopying, recording or by means of any information storage or retrieval system without prior permission in writing from the publishers; or ii) used or reproduced in any way for the training, development or operation of artificial intelligence (AI) technologies, including generative AI technologies. The rights holders expressly reserve this publication from the text and data mining exception as per Article 4(3) of the Digital Single Market Directive (EU) 2019/790

A catalogue record for this book is available from the British Library.

ISBN: PB 9781472868435; eBook 9781472868442; ePDF 9781472868411; XML 9781472868428

26 27 28 29 30   10 9 8 7 6 5 4 3 2 1

Maps by Bounford.com
3D BEVs by Paul Kime
Index by Mark Swift
Typeset by Lumina Datamatics Ltd
Printed by Repro India Ltd

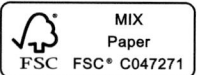

Author's note

Translating out of Cyrillic always poses challenges. I have chosen to transliterate names as they are pronounced, and have also ignored the diacritical 'soft' and 'hard' signs found in the original. The only exceptions are names that have acquired common forms in English and 'Ivan the Terrible' rather than 'Ivan Grozny'. I will generally use the Russian plural form ending in -i or -y, again unless there is some customary English form (such as 'tsars' or 'boyars'). Likewise, I try to render Tatar names and terms in the most generally recognizable forms, but there are multiple options, and my apologies for any inconsistencies. Russians are the people largely within the state that is Muscovy, and likewise the peoples of the Kazan, Crimean and other khanates are Tatars.

On dates, I generally use the Julian calendar used at the time rather than modern dating under the Gregorian calendar, so that for example the fall of Kazan, which is commemorated on 15 October these days, is given as 2 October.

Glossary

Boyar	Member of the established, landed Muscovite aristocracy [Russian]
Chambul	Detached raiding party [Tatar]
Dyeti boyarskiye	Lesser aristocrats, lit. 'boyar children' [Russian]
Kremlin	Castle [Russian]
Murza	Hereditary aristocrat [Tatar]
Pishchal	Matchlock arquebus, although sometimes used for larger guns [Russian]
Pischalnik	Arquebusier, plural *pishchalniki* [Russian]
Polk	Regiment; plural *polki* [Russian]
Pomeshchik	Member of the Muscovite gentry, granted land in exchange for service, plural *pomeshchiki* [Russian]
Posad	Walled neighbourhood [Russian]
Pososhnye lyudi	'Assembled people', labour militia [Russian]
Sotnia	'Hundred', company; plural, *soten* [Russian]
Sotnik	Commander of a *sotnia* [Russian]
Strelets	'Musketeer', member of first Russian standing army; plural *Streltsy* [Russian]
Tsar	Emperor, a title that came to supersede grand prince [Russian]
Tyufyak	Small, early cannon [Russian]
Ulus	Tribe or nation [Tatar]
Voivode	Governor or military commander [Russian]

Osprey Publishing supports the Woodland Trust, the UK's leading woodland conservation charity.

To find out more about our authors and books visit www.ospreypublishing.com. Here you will find extracts, author interviews, details of forthcoming events and the option to sign up for our newsletter.

For product safety related questions contact productsafety@bloomsbury.com

Front cover main illustration: The final defence, 2 October 1552. (Angel García Pinto)
Title page photograph: Muscovite light cavalry scour the Kazan countryside for Tatar raiders, forage and plunder. (Bildagentur-online/Universal Images Group via Getty Images)

CONTENTS

ORIGINS OF THE CAMPAIGN 4
The Khanate of Kazan . A history of conflict . Ivan's early campaigns

CHRONOLOGY 21

OPPOSING COMMANDERS 22
Muscovy . Kazan

OPPOSING FORCES 27
Muscovy . Kazan

OPPOSING PLANS 46
Muscovy . Kazan

THE CAMPAIGN 52
Archa and Kama . Laying siege . By mine and cannon . The assault . Endgame

AFTERMATH 77
Guerrilla war, 1552–56 . The conquest of Astrakhan . Great power, great rivals

THE BATTLEFIELD TODAY 89

FURTHER READING 93

INDEX 95

ORIGINS OF THE CAMPAIGN

> I sing of Russia liberated from the barbarians,
> the Tatar power trampled and pride overthrown, the
> movement of ancient forces, labours, bloody battles,
> the triumph of Russia, the destruction of Kazan.
> From the circle of these times, the beginning of calm years.
> Like a bright dawn, it shone in Russia.

The introduction to Mikhail Kheraskov's pompous epic poem the *Rossiyada*, a 10,000-verse work written in the late 18th century, was intended to remind Russians of their heroic past and frame the 1552 capture of Kazan as a pivotal moment in their story. As a historical source it is deeply flawed, but as a symbol of the genuine importance of this engagement it is priceless.

Ivan Vasilievich, who became grand prince of Moscow and all Russia in 1533, at the age of just three, would become the first ruler of Muscovy to be crowned tsar in 1547. As Ivan IV, he would acquire the epithet *Grozny*, generally translated as 'the Terrible', even if in fact 'the Awesome' is perhaps closest to its sense of a man of capacities beyond the usual. In many ways, his would be a reign shaped not just by the ambitions of Ivan as a monarch – for he played a key role in shaping the institutions of the emerging Russian

Moscow had long been in the thrall first of the Golden Horde and then its successor khanates, and its rise was marked by its progressive defiance of the Tatars. Here, Grand Prince Ivan III – Ivan the Great – is refusing to pay tribute to Kazan in 1480 and, in 1487, would briefly manage to force the khanate to pay tribute to Moscow. (Sovfoto/Universal Images Group via Getty Images)

state – but also his fears. Along with coup and conspiracy by the boyars (aristocrats), whose intrigues had shaped the regency during his minority, he was keenly aware of the threats he faced from abroad. To the west was the Grand Duchy of Lithuania, one of the great military powers of the age, with whom Muscovy had fought a series of wars. To the south and east, though, were the khanates formed by the break-up of the Mongol-Tatar Golden Horde, which had conquered most of the cities of the Rus' in the 13th century and claimed suzerainty over them until the reign of his grandfather, Ivan III, in the late 15th century. These periodically raided the Russians for plunder and, especially, captives – Crimea became a crucial market for slaves sold to the Ottoman Empire. Indeed, the Crimeans nearly took Moscow in 1521 and continued to be able to project forces into the very Russian heartland for another century.

THE KHANATE OF KAZAN

The Khanate of Kazan was one of the greatest of the Turkic successor states to the Golden Horde, formed on the territory of the Bulgar Ulus when Ulugh Muhammad ('Muhammad the Older') lost his position atop the Horde following a dynastic struggle. He fled to the ulus or lands of the Volga Bulgars in 1437, where he captured the existing city of Kazan the following year, declaring himself the khan of a new, independent nation, which he ruled until his death in 1445. Successive khans would see Kazan grow in wealth and power, not least by raiding the lands of the Russians. As early as 1439, Ulugh Muhammad had besieged Moscow, and, while he retreated after 11 days, he had plundered Kolomna, Ryazan and other Russian towns on the way. In 1444, he even captured Grand Duke Vasily II of Moscow, demanding a huge ransom for his release. His successors extended the khanate's territories east and north-east, into the lands of the Udmurts and eventually as far as the Ural Mountains, while still pressing Muscovy.

Kazan's particular curse was to have to navigate between the age's two dominant powers of the region, Muscovy and the Crimean Khanate.

The city of Kazan had become a wealthy, cosmopolitan trading centre, but many Tatars in the countryside still lived very traditional lifestyles. (Bettmann/Getty Images)

Kazan had emerged as a major political and economic centre since the late 13th century, but it lacked the muscle of either, and thus often survived by playing one off against the other. In 1512, for example, the rather optimistically and unrealistically named Treaty of Eternal Peace and Unbreakable Friendship between Kazan and Moscow was signed by Grand Duke Vasily III and Khan Muhammad-Emin. However, after the khan's death, Kazan was soon joining the Crimean Khanate in a massive attack on Moscow. Likewise, individuals and factions within Kazan's elite would often align themselves with either power – and, indeed, other polities such as the Nogai Khanate – such that some even regard Ivan the Terrible's conquest as an intervention into a Tatar civil war as much as an act of Russian imperialism.

The Zilant, or Ajdaha, has become a symbol of Kazan, and may have come originally from the mythologies of the Volga Bulgar. Here a modern statue of this winged serpent stands before the Kazan Kremlin walls and the Kul Sharif Mosque. (© Mark Galeotti)

The khan was nominally an absolute ruler, but in practice was often at the mercy of both the Kazan mob and also the powerful magnates who sat on the *divan*, the council of nobles, as well as the *kurultai*, a larger assembly that might be convened at times of particular crisis, and which also included representatives from landowners, military commanders and the clergy. Although the khan did have his personal forces, paid for with the revenues of tribute and his own lands, for any major operation, he had to turn to the *begs*, governors of cities and regions, and the feudal aristocracy of the *murzas* and the *oghlans*, who could very loosely be compared to the boyars and service gentry of the Muscovite state.

The city of Kazan

Founded at the start of the 11th century, Kazan means 'cauldron' in both Tatar and Russian. In myth, this happened when a sorcerer told a leader of the Bulgars to found a city where a cauldron would boil water when simply dug into the ground, which led them to the confluence of two rivers: the Volga and the Kazanka. Under Ulugh Muhammad Khan and his successors, it would expand from its early status as little more than a fortified river town into a city and regional trading hub on the Great Volga Route, attracting merchants from as far as Bukhara, who flocked to an international fair held annually on what became known as Guest Island.

The riches brought by this trade were in part invested in increasingly capable defences. Prince Andrei Kurbsky, one of Ivan's most trusted allies and later one of his most outspoken critics, described his first impressions on approaching it in his *History of the Grand Duke of Moscow*. While he had every reason to talk up Kazan's impregnability, not least to highlight his own martial feats in the subsequent battle, it nonetheless represents one of the best outsider's perspectives at our disposal:

> And then we neared the city of Kazan, which is located in the most inaccessible terrain: to the east of it flows the Kazanka River and, to the west, the river of Bulak, very swamped and impassable. It runs right beneath the city and, by the Corner Tower, flows into the Kazanka River … And, if you succeed in crossing this river, which is a very difficult task, then between the city and the [Kaban] lake from the direction of the Arsk [Archa] field, you see a very steep and unassailable mountain. And around the city, from that river to the little lake called Unclear, a very deep moat is dug. And from the Kazan River, the hill is so high that it is barely possible to encompass it with your sight. Upon the hill, there are the fortress and the tsar's [khan's] palace, and the tall stone mosques, where their deceased kings are buried. As I recall, they are five in number…

Accounts of the city suggest it was unfortified in the mid-15th century, when in 1469, Muscovite voivode (governor) Ivan Runo, in defiance of Grand Duke Ivan III's orders, launched a successful raid on the city, burning down some of its outer suburbs and withdrawing with freed Russian slaves and considerable booty. In 1500, Khan Ghabdellatif built a prison on the city's outskirts, and these in due course would anchor the first walls when, in 1530, Khan Safa Giray decreed that, 'near the settlement along the Archa field, from Bulak to the Kazanka, dig ditches around it, behind the prison'. By 1549, the city was surrounded by walls (described later), with ten gates around them.

Within those walls was a thriving settlement of 10,000–15,000 citizens, up to twice the size of Saray-Jük, capital of the Nogai Khanate, and larger than Astrakhan. On the western bank of the Bulak River was the city's main market square, between the Crimean Gate and Tashayak (Stone Bowl) Street. Along the banks of the slow-flowing Bulak were artisans' workshops,

Outside the walls, some settlements led right up to the Kazanka and Bulak Rivers, despite the marshiness of the terrain, which would also impede Russian attacks during the siege. (DEA/BIBLIOTECA AMBROSIANA/Getty Images)

Much of the history of the siege of Kazan has to be pieced together from archaeological finds as well as the rival claims of often biased and exaggerated sources, of which arguably the most implausible is the *Kazan Chronicle*. (Unknown author, CC BY-SA 4.0 https://creativecommons.org/licenses/by-sa/4.0, via Wikimedia Commons)

especially potteries and metalworkers. All of this city was characterized by close-set and essentially unplanned development, such that contemporaries complained that it was all but impossible to ride a horse away from the main streets, something that would make fighting through this densely packed environment a bloody and difficult task for the Russians.

In the northern part of the city was the Khan's Palace, which, like a typical Russian kremlin, was a fortified complex of buildings rather than a single stricture. This dated back to the 10th century and included the actual palace of the sovereign, the city's main mosques (including the white-stone Kul Sharif Mosque, famed for its size and beauty), as well as several smaller ones, barracks, storehouses and the homes of the wealthier magnates of the city. From its main gate, a wide road led to the Khan's Gate in the outer walls, the central thoroughfare of the city.

Outside Kazan's walls were a handful of other settlements, especially those to which foreigners were confined. There was a separate Armenians' village south of the city, for example, while Bishbalta, to the north-west on the banks of the Kazanka, had formed around wharfs and shipbuilders' workshops. To the south-west were the Khan's Meadows, used in summer for festivals and horse races.

A HISTORY OF CONFLICT

Russian sources in particular tend to explain the conflict between Moscow and Kazan in essentially defensive terms: that the emerging state of Muscovy had to defend itself from Tatar slave-taking raids in the immediate term, and the threat of a rising Ottoman Empire – which was happy to bring the khanates under its wing – in the long term. This is all perfectly true, and was compounded by the bad blood created by over a century of mutual attacks. The Kazan Khanate, like the Crimean, was especially dependent on the wealth generated by raiding for and trading slaves, all but forcing it to maintain an aggressive posture towards the Russians and lesser communities under their

Muscovy and its neighbours, 1552

Although this etching shrinks the formidable composite bow used by the Tatars into a toy, the Crimean Tatars would remain a distinctive force and feared warriors into the 18th century. (Bildagentur-online/Universal Images Group via Getty Images)

protection. Collating the claims in chronicles and other primary documents with archaeological evidence, it is possible to state, for example, that there was at least one substantial raid from Kazan each year in the span 1534–45, and this was probably not untypical.

Sometimes, it was Kazan that had the upper hand, at others, it was Muscovy – which claimed, but rarely could enforce, the right to appoint the khans – who would be victorious; in 1530, Ivan's father Vasily III put the city to the torch, ousted Khan Safa Giray, and replaced him with Dzhan Ali, ruler of the Qasim Khanate, a vassal state of Moscow's. He was never an especially dominant figure, though, and in 1535, after Vasily's death, he was toppled in a palace coup and Safa Giray was restored to the throne. Members of the nobility considered too close to the Russians fled Kazan, and Safa Giray looked for revenge. Kazan was again arming for war. In 1536, armies from both sides held a tense stand-off near the village of Lyskovo, some 50 miles east of the Russian city of Nizhny Novgorod, but neither side pressed battle: the Russians were outnumbered, but the Tatars had counted on surprise. The next year, though, a large force pushed to and past Nizhny Novgorod, swinging north up the Volga towards Kostroma. There, they routed a Russian army, killing the voivode of Kostroma Prince Pyotr Zasekin. The Tatars pressed south to the fortress town of Murom, but this held and, as winter pressed on their supply lines, they settled for burning the outskirts of the town and retreating to Nizhny Novgorod.

The regents ruling Muscovy in Ivan's name (as he was not yet of age) initially planned a counterattack, but Safa Giray's uncle, Saip Giray, had become khan of Crimea with the backing of the Ottoman Empire. Fearing that an attack on Kazan would leave them vulnerable to the Crimeans, they instead opened negotiations. These only gave Safa Giray time to regroup, though, and confirmed him in his belief that they had little stomach for a fight. In 1539, the Tatars again attacked Murom and raided settlements across a wide front, as far north as Galich. The Russians had been preparing, however, and their forces, supported by the Qasim Khanate's, met the main Tatar army at Plyos, south-east of Kostroma. It was a hard battle,

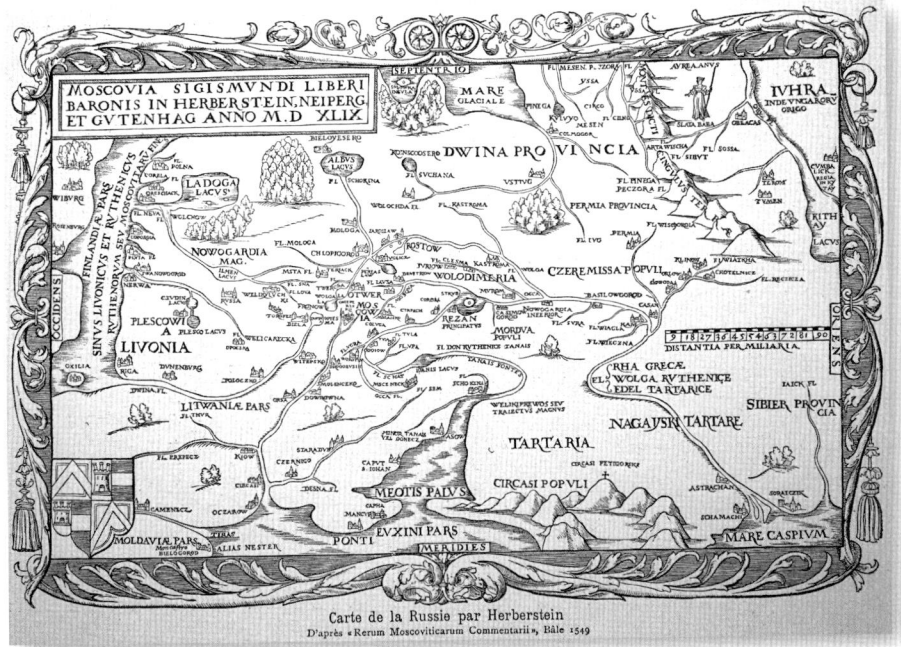

A map of Muscovy published by the German diplomat Sigismund von Herberstein in 1549. Kazan – spelled 'Casan' – is to the east of Moscow, on the fringes of 'Tartaria'. (World History Archive/Alamy)

but ultimately the Tatars broke, leaving their captives and their booty, and withdrew to Kazan.

A constant headache to Muscovy was the need to consider not just the threat from the khanates to the south and east but also the Grand Duchy of Lithuania to the north-west. After the Fifth Lithuanian–Muscovite War of 1534–37, they had agreed a five-year truce that would later be extended. The Russians could thus begin to concentrate their forces to the south. Again, the Crimeans would delay their plans. In 1541, they invaded, apparently convinced by the turncoat Prince Semyon Belsky that the Russians had already begun moving on Kazan. They were met on the Oka River south of Moscow by so large a force (coincidentally led by Semyon's elder brother, Prince Dmitry) that Saip Giray withdrew without battle, complaining to Belsky that 'you told me that the Grand Duke's people were going to Kazan, that I would not be met, but I have never seen so many well-dressed people in one place' – 'well-dressed', needless to say, meaning well-armed and -armoured.

Nonetheless, this had delayed the Russians, and their long-awaited campaign against Kazan only began in 1545. Three detachments converged on the city, with the plan being that this would coincide with a coup by pro-Russian elements. When this failed, the attackers, who lacked the siege train to take such a well-defended city, were forced to withdraw. One of the detachments, which had marched from Perm under Prince Lvov, was attacked and decimated, while Safa Giray launched a campaign of repressions at home. His enemies, in desperation, finally launched their coup in January 1546. Safa Giray fled and solicited aid from the Astrakhan Khanate, but his successor, Shigalei, overplayed his hand by inviting Muscovy to send troops to hold the city in his name. The Kazan crowd turned against him, closing the gates on the Russians and forcing Shigalei to flee, and a month later, Safa Giray was back in power, his enemies dead or in exile (no fewer than four princes of Kazan fled to Moscow), his Crimean allies holding key government positions, and his mood angrier than ever.

The Kazan Khanate, 1500

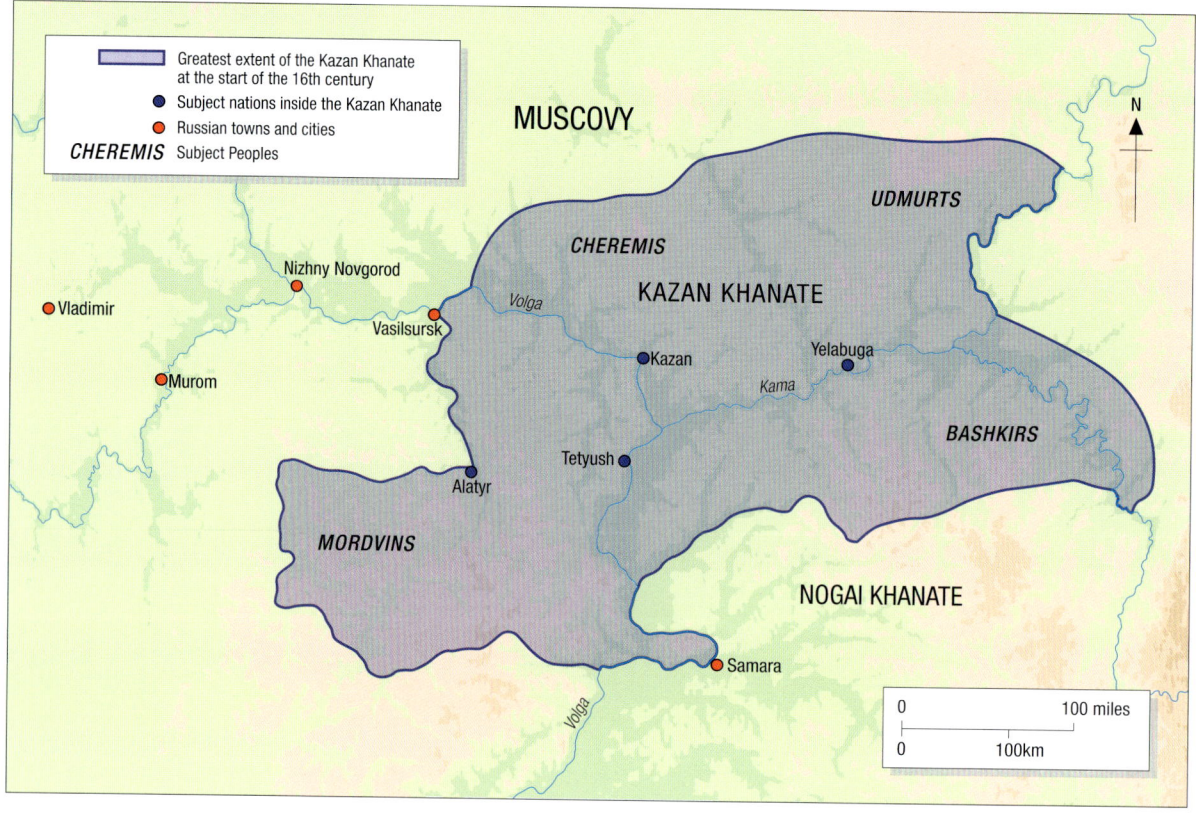

Russian ambitions

However, retribution for over a century of slaving raids was by no means the only factor behind the invasion. Kazan posed a threat to Muscovite trade along the Volga River, one of the great transport arteries of the age. Far more importantly, Ivan needed land. The rise of Muscovy had been fuelled by its dynasty's capacity to bring more territories under its control and use the consequent revenues for further expansion. With the Russian principalities essentially all taken (wealthy Novgorod was annexed by Ivan III in 1478), there was a reason to look elsewhere for additional territories and riches to buy off the boyars and endow a new generation of service gentry, the *pomeshchiki*. Unlike the boyars, who inherited their lands, the gentry were awarded them in exchange for service. The *pomeshchiki* increasingly made up the backbone of the Muscovite army and officialdom – and also Ivan trusted (insofar as he trusted anyone) service gentry beholden to him more than the boyar families who had used him as a puppet during his regency. If he wanted to expand his army, build up his state apparatus and strengthen the counterweight to boyar power, a tsar needed more land to distribute, and this generally meant conquest. Ivan Peresvetov, who championed the interests of the gentry over the boyars, urged Ivan IV to 'send daring warriors to the Kazan lands and order them to burn and ravage and take captive the people' because of its wealth, and warned the young tsar that its khan was his 'worst enemy'.

As well as these practical reasons, Ivan also had a religious and ideological reason for moving against Kazan. Although there is no real basis for seeing the conflict as primarily driven by tensions between

Orthodox Christianity and Islam, both sides certainly used this as a pretext to push their own agendas. Since 1520, the Crimean Khanate had tried to mobilize this in order to win the support of the Ottomans for its claim over Kazan. Then, Khan Mehmed I Giray claimed (falsely) that thanks to Russian influence, mosques in Kazan were being destroyed and churches built in their place. Moscow's envoy to Istanbul had to earnestly argue the case to Sultan Selim I that none of this was true. However, there were those in Moscow who would wish it to be true. The priest Sylvester, one of Ivan's closest advisors, was a strong supporter of efforts to push back Islam. In around 1550, he presented the pious and superstitious young tsar with a mishmash of doctored quotations from scripture to try and persuade him that it was foreseen that, with divine favour, he was destined to break the power of the 'pagan tsars'.

IVAN'S EARLY CAMPAIGNS

In 1547, the 16-year-old Ivan was crowned tsar. After a regency in which he had felt taken for granted and underestimated, he was determined to make his mark. He also saw this as a moment in which it was time to end the threat from Kazan for once and for all – and also a chance to acquire more territory to endow more *pomeshchiki* and reduce his dependence on the boyars. Young, over-confident and mistrustful of his court, Ivan decided to lead a campaign against Kazan personally, setting off from Vladimir in the winter of that year. Typically, in deep winter, the frozen rivers were crucial transport arteries down which cannon and sleds of supplies could be dragged with relative ease. However, this proved an unexpectedly wet and mild season. From the first, it was hard to move the army's cannon because the ground was thick with mud, and when the army encamped on the island of Robotka, on the frozen Volga River east of Nizhny Novgorod, they awoke on 4 February 1548 to a calamity. In the words of the *Nikon Chronicle*, 'by some act of God, it grew warm and a thaw came, and all the ice was covered with water'. When they tried to ford their way to the banks of the river, 'many cannons and guns fell into the water… And many people drowned'. At this point, Ivan returned to Nizhny Novgorod, 'shedding many tears' according to the chronicle. Although his army battled on to reach Kazan later that month, without its siege guns and exhausted by struggling through mud and rain, it could not muster a serious challenge to the city's defences. They stayed encamped around the city for a week, as much to rest as to save face, before Prince Dmitry Belsky, their commander, ordered them to head back for home.

In March 1549, Safa Giray died suddenly, leaving his two-year-old son Utamish Giray as notional khan and Safa Giray's widow, the Nogai princess Söyembikä, as regent. This was an unstable situation, and Söyembikä's loyalties were suspect for the pro-Crimean hardliners, especially after she had offered Ivan peace negotiations. This faction hurriedly sent an appeal to Saip Giray for assistance in imposing a new khan or regent from their number. However, the envoys were apparently all intercepted by Cossack mercenaries in Moscow's service and so the opportunity to, in effect, stage a pro-Crimean coup was missed. In any case, for Ivan, Söyembikä's overtures were a sign of weakness, and he resolved to make another attempt to deal with Kazan.

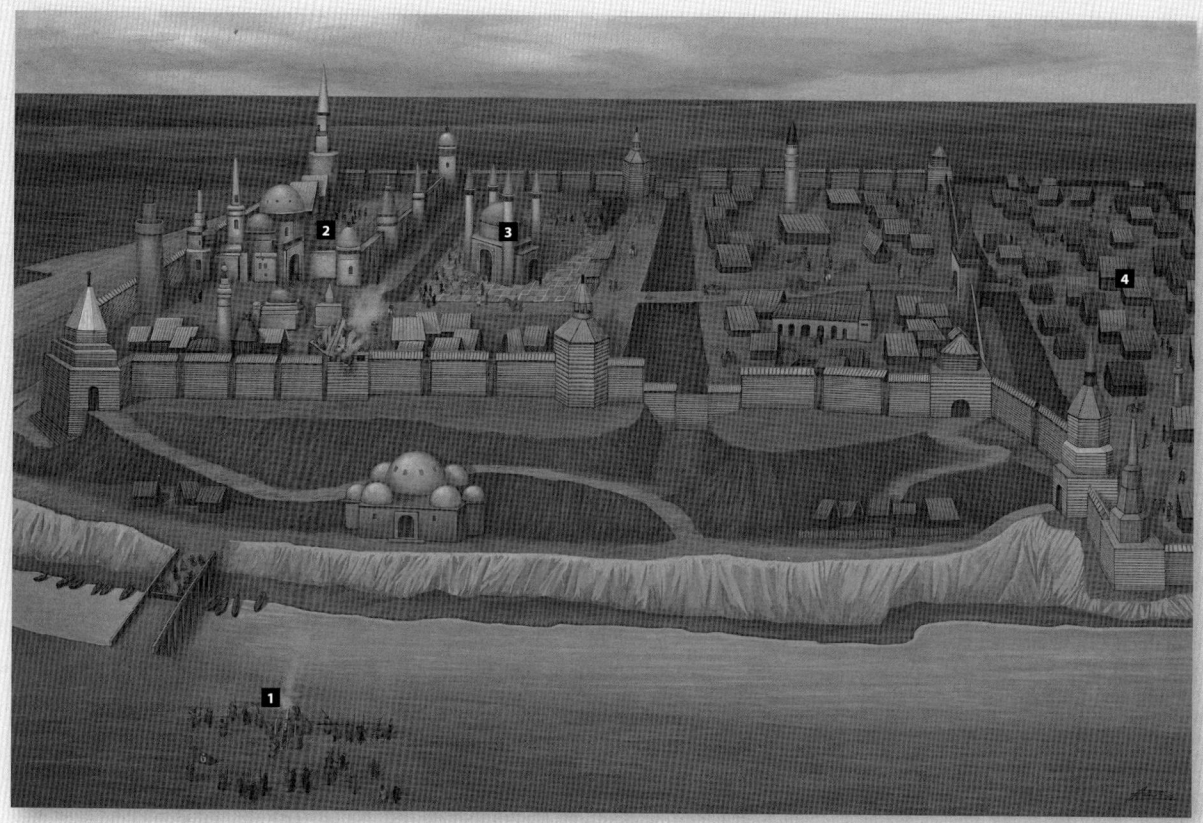

SIEGE OF KAZAN, FEBRUARY 1548 (PP.14–15)

By the time what was left of the Muscovite army reached Kazan in February 1548, their failure was essentially a foregone conclusion, and the resulting week-long siege was just a *pro forma* engagement to preserve some shred of honour. Here, one of the few Russian guns that made it to Kazan has been emplaced **(1)** on the far bank of the Bulak River and is engaged in a desultory bombardment of the Khan's Palace so long as its supplies of gunpowder last. In order to prevent it from being attacked by Kazan cavalry, it is being guarded by a small detachment of spearmen from Yaroslavl, flying its design of a black bear holding a poleaxe. The palace itself is a separate walled compound to the north of the city, containing the actual palace of the khan and the barracks of his personal retinue **(2)** and the city's main mosque **(3)**, cut off from the main body of the city **(4)**.

At the start of 1550, ignoring these offers of negotiation, Ivan led a renewed campaign against Kazan. This time, his luck seemed better and his forces swept aside the Tatar pickets and settled into a siege of the city in February. Once again, though, mild weather would be his undoing. His siege lines were pelted with heavy rain, and high winds made aiming his guns all the harder. The chronicle recounted that 'the winds were strong, and the rains were great, and the mud was immeasurable; and the cannons and arquebuses were impotent, and it was not possible to approach the city for mud'. The early thaw also hindered reinforcement and resupply, especially as independent tribes along the Volga would raid supply boats, and raised the threat that his heavy artillery would be bogged down in the thick mud. Hopes that the surviving elements of the pro-Moscow faction would rise in support also came to nothing. After 11 days, Ivan lifted the siege and returned home.

It was not a total defeat, though. While the work that became known as the *Zafar nama-yi wilayat-i Qazan*, *The Victory Book of the Kazan Khanate*, portrays this as a heroic and crushing victory by Kazan, it was really the result of poor planning and bad luck. Moscow's forces were essentially intact and could be mobilized again. Besides, Kazan's hinterland had been ravaged and looted, and its economy took a corresponding hit.

A Russian re-enactor showing the typical uniform and equipment of Ivan's elite musketeers. (Mihail Siergiejevicz/SOPA Images/LightRocket via Getty Images)

Furthermore, on the way back, Ivan paused at the confluence of the Sviyaga and Volga Rivers, and according to the chronicles God inspired him to build a fortress there. Whether divine or earthly inspiration, this was a shrewd move, and it would provide both a fortified advance base and logistical hub for future operations as well as a clear expression of Moscow's determination to extend its authority down the Volga. It was important to build it quickly, not least to prevent Kazan from launching an attack to disrupt operations, so in April 1551, Prince Yuri Bulgakov-Golitsyn led an army of Muscovite troops and Tatar allies, with a sizeable force of carpenters and labourers, to the site. While Pyotr Serebryany-Obolensky ravaged the lands of Kazan as a distraction with a force of Cossacks moving by riverboat, construction of the fort began – and was essentially completed within a month. This feat was possible thanks not only to the ever-present fear of disappointing the energetic and ruthless new tsar but also Russians' traditional skill in woodcrafting. The fortress, which was christened Sviyazhsk, was perhaps the world's first prefabricated castle, built in sections upstream at Uglich, each numbered and accompanied by a plan

The fortress of Sviyazhsk

Built atop Kruglaya Hill, the fortress was even larger than the Moscow Kremlin at the time. It comprised a round enclosed bastion (the kremlin) within a wider log-walled town (the *posad*) oval in plan. Its oaken walls were made up of the distinctive architectural unit known as the *goroden*, a cubic or rectangular structure of interlocking logs that was then filled with earth. Some 420 of them made up a wall 1.6 miles in circumference, between 16 wooden towers, of which five were gatehouses. Fully half the wooden construction was made up of the prefabricated pieces shipped from Uglich, the rest, including the logs used for the outer wall, was cut from the surrounding forests. The *posad* would soon be crowded with houses and churches, but at first Sviyazhsk was primarily a military settlement, with a Granary Yard and a State Yard, where gunpowder and cannonballs were stored. Outside the walls was a path leading down to a pier on the Sviyaga River, where a separate settlement soon sprang up. Despite its hasty construction, the fort lasted for over a century before it started to collapse, not least because of subsidence. It was rebuilt, but as the threat from Kazan and the khanates was now over, the new fortifications were substantially weaker, with the wall replaced with a simple stockade and just four towers. When the Kuibyshev Reservoir on the Volga was completed in 1955–57, the water level rose significantly, and the lowland *posad* part of Sviyazhsk was flooded, leaving the hilltop where the kremlin had stood as an island.

showing how it fitted together. They were then floated down the river to be assembled. Unlike so much modern flatpack furniture, it worked.

Many of the indigenous Volga peoples, who survived by recognizing which way the wind was blowing, were impressed by this Muscovite show of force. In particular, the so-called 'Mountain Cheremis' (now more often known as Mari), who lived on the hillier left bank of the Volga, petitioned to become vassals of the tsar. In the words of the chronicle, 'the mountain people, seeing that the city of the Orthodox Tsar had become part of their land, began to come to the Tsar and petition that the sovereign would grant them favour, give up his anger, and order his governors to stay near the city of Sviyazhsk and not to fight them'. This, Ivan was very happy to do: not only did it satisfy his vanity and his need to demonstrate success, it also secured his supply lines for his next campaign and provided him with additional scouts and warriors. Along with the Mountain Cheremis, the Mordvins and the Chuvash were also welcomed and granted concessions and gifts in return for their promises of fealty (promises that would prove reliable only so long as Moscow seemed in the ascendant).

The construction of Sviyazhsk, Serebryany-Obolensky's raids and the defection of the 'Mountainside' Volga peoples also shocked Kazan, and led to another of the regular and ephemeral changes in power. Having failed to act in 1550, the pro-Moscow faction, sensing the dismay of their rivals, struck. Thanks to the passive support of figures who were not so much pro-Moscow as eager to avoid a war, they were successful and asked Ivan's terms. Following negotiations, Utamish Giray, Söyembikä and some 60,000 Russian slaves were handed over, and the former khan, Shigalei, was installed as their new ruler. Shigalei was already regarded with some suspicion in Kazan as being too close to Moscow – he had been a favourite of Vasily III – and when he turned up in August 1551 with a guard of not just 300

Russian cavalry, probably *pomeshchiki*, in *tegilyai* quilted caftans and bearing both bows and the sword-bladed cavalry spears that would later be called the *sovnya*, but which seemed to have no special name at the time. (Public domain via Wikimedia Commons)

Establishing the island fortress of Sviyazhsk, which soon grew into a town in its own right, would prove a crucial step towards securing the supply lines for operations down the Volga against Kazan and later Astrakhan. (Engraving based on a drawing by M. I. Makhaev [mid-18th century], public domain, via Wikimedia Commons)

men from the Qasim Khanate, but 200 Muscovite arquebusiers and the Muscovite emissaries Ivan Khabarov and Ivan Vyrodkov, rumours began to spread that he was going to hand power over to a Russian governor. Conspirators tried unsuccessfully to persuade the Nogai Khanate to intervene, and although Shigalei was able to quell this plot, Ivan became increasingly demanding, not least of full title to the 'Mountainside' Volga region, because he had 'taken its inhabitants by sabre before their petition'. When the khan refused to allow Moscow to send more of its own troops to guard the city, fearing that the Crimean Khanate and its Ottoman allies might use this as a pretext to intervene, rumour became reality as some Russians began arguing that Shigalei was insufficiently obedient and ought to be replaced with a governor. In early 1552, Prince Semyon Mikulinsky, a seasoned soldier and administrator, was chosen for the role even though the tsar did not yet have this kind of authority over the city. Too independent for Moscow, too supine for the Kazan mob, in March 1552 Shigalei fled the city, fearing – with good reason – an armed rising. Mikulinsky sent emissaries to Kazan demanding that the notables of the city prepare to swear their allegiance. He then headed for Kazan, but amidst fervid talk that he planned a massacre or enforced conversion to Christianity, crowds closed the gates to him, and he was forced to return to Sviyazhsk in dishonour and disarray.

Meanwhile, as the people of Kazan acclaimed a new khan, Prince Ediger-Magmet from Astrakhan (who claimed direct descent from Genghis Khan), with the blessing of the Nogai Khanate, and Ivan, according to the *Kazan Chronicle*, 'repented that he had made peace with the Kazan people, and for many days he remained in sorrow, and no one could console him in his deep sorrow', the Russians received yet more bad news. The Mountain Cheremis had swapped sides again, declaring for Kazan, while the ambitious new Crimean Khan Devlet Giray was on the march. His Tatars were this time supported by Turkish Janissaries, and they were already attacking Tula, whose walls were being battered by Ottoman guns. The Crimean threat was soon defused, as a Muscovite relief column quickly forced them into disorderly retreat, abandoning their supply train and guns (several of

The siege of Tula, June 1552

In 1551, Khan Saip Giray had fallen foul of the Ottoman Sultan Suleiman I by refusing to provide forces for an attack on Persia and had been replaced by his cousin Devlet Giray. Devlet needed to prove his mettle, and with both him and the Ottomans eager to disrupt the Muscovite campaign against Kazan, he opted to march into the Ryazan region and thence to Kolomna, south-east of Moscow. The idea was that this would force Ivan to divert his forces, and leave the Crimeans well placed to push further into Russia. In June 1552, learning that Ivan's army was already mustering along the Oka River, Devlet Giray – who was looking to stage a raid in force rather than an open battle with a fully mobilized Russian army – opted to divert to Tula, further west, not least in the hope of gaining plunder with which to buy his new army's loyalties. On 21 June, Crimean outriders reached Tula, but found its gates closed and its garrison forearmed. The Russian forces under Prince Grigory Temkin-Rostovsky were too few to challenge the Crimeans in the field, but could instead rely on the city's robust defences, which included a stone kremlin and high, well-built wooden walls studded with nine towers armed with cannon.

The next day, the main body of Devlet's 30,000-strong army reached Tula, including Turkish Janissaries and 17 heavy siege guns. They immediately began bombarding the city with cannonballs that had been heated in fires to become incendiaries, and the city's inhabitants were pressed into service fighting the fires while the soldiers manned the walls to repel an attempt to storm them by the Janissaries. Although one of the city's gates was breached, the attack was unsuccessful and repelled with heavy casualties. Meanwhile, news had reached Ivan at Kolomna, and he quickly dispatched a strong relief force of more than 10,000 men under Pyotr Shchenyatev and Andrei Kurbsky, with the rest of his army following more slowly.

On Thursday 23 June, the Crimeans were launching a renewed assault when word began to spread about the approach of the relief force. The tale grew in the telling until it was being rumoured that it was the entire Muscovite army, with Ivan at its head. With no prospect of a quick seizure of the city, and with his brother-in-law falling in the attack, Devlet Giray decided to withdraw. The Tula garrison, supported by the city's militia, sortied from the city, and the withdrawal became increasingly disorderly, with the precious siege guns being abandoned, along with much loot that had been gathered during the advance. Then the advancing Muscovite force was able to engage the Crimeans on the banks of the Shivoron River, and although outnumbered, took advantage of their enemies' disorganization to deliver a further serious blow that sent Devlet into full-scale retreat, abandoning mounts, captives and the wounded. He would be unable to provide any help for Kazan when it was besieged and posed no more threat to Muscovy until 1555. By the time he heard the news, Ivan was at Kashira, halfway between Tula and Kolomna. He led his retinue in prayers of thanks, returned to Kolomna, and gave the army a week's rest before it was time to march on Kazan.

which would later be put to use against Kazan), as well as herds of camels. Nonetheless, in some ways it was the very seriousness of the situation that made Ivan rise to the moment. His spine stiffened by a sermon from Makary, Metropolitan of Moscow, that his was as much a spiritual as secular war against the infidel, he was determined to end the threat from Kazan once and for all.

A recurring nightmare for Moscow was the intrusion of Ottoman power into the region, through and in alliance with the Crimeans. Elite Janissaries such as the figure on the left, as well as artillerymen, would increasingly accompany Crimean Tatars on their raids against Moscow. (Sepia Times/Universal Images Group via Getty Images)

CHRONOLOGY

1533	Ivan IV crowned grand prince (at age of three)		July: Ivan sets off for Kazan
1537	Khanate of Kazan launches attack on Murom		15 August: Muscovite forces cross Volga
1539	Renewed assault on Murom		23 August: Kazan forces launch sortie
1547	January: Ivan IV crowned tsar		24 August: Battle of Archa
1548	February: Muscovite forces besiege Kazan, then withdraw		27 August: Siege of Kazan begins
			4 September: Water Gate mined
1549	March: Death of Khan Safa Giray		26 September: Sortie against the siege tower
1550	January: Second Kazan Campaign launched		2 October: Kazan stormed
	February: Muscovite forces besiege Kazan, then withdraw		11 October: Ivan leaves for Moscow
	Streltsy formed	**1552–56**	Kazan guerrilla war
1551	Founding of Sviyazhsk	**1556**	Conquest of Astrakhan Khanate
	Shigalei installed as khan	**1569**	Abortive Crimean siege of Astrakhan
1552	March: Shigalei flees Kazan; Mikulinsky denied entry; Ediger-Magmet acclaimed as new khan	**1571**	Crimeans burn Moscow
		1572	Crimeans defeated in Battle of Molodi
	June: Ivan musters forces at Kolomna for Third Kazan Campaign; Crimeans besiege and are then driven from Tula		

The siege of Kazan was the first true triumph both of Moscow's emerging artillery and its new corps of professional *Streltsy*, or 'musketeers'. Here a historical re-enactor in the uniform of a *Strelets* stands by a later cannon. His distinctive *berdysh* poleaxe, propped against the cannon, also doubled as a stand for his firearm. (Mihail Siergiejevicz/SOPA Images/LightRocket via Getty Images)

OPPOSING COMMANDERS

He says: Prepare to blossom, Russian state!
The pious spirit of the Tsar leads to Kazan;
The capital city awaits him with a thunderous splash.
The Almighty inclined his eye towards him
And the Tsar solemnly entered his capital;
– *Rossiyada*

MUSCOVY

Ivan IV, Ivan Grozny, in his royal regalia, in an etching from shortly before his death in 1584. (Rischgitz/Getty Images)

Tsar Ivan IV was something of a paradox: intelligent, even far-sighted, yet brooding and prone to bouts of paranoid violence that only became more dominant as he aged, perhaps as a result of the pain he experienced from progressive bone diseases and the mercury he took in the hope of a cure. His childhood left him scarred, with his father dying when he was just three years old and his mother, possibly by poisoning, when he was eight. There followed a regency in which the boyar Shuisky and Belsky families vied for control, while the young figurehead, even while clad in cloth of gold for state events, was neglected and brutalized, even having to scavenge for scraps from the kitchens. Yet as he grew into his majority, he would take bloody revenge: even at the age of 13, he had a prince who offended him beaten to death, and later he would have many boyars killed, exiled or imprisoned. Crowned tsar at 16, he led his first, abortive, campaign against Kazan that same year. It failed, but he proved quick to learn, not least to rely on his experienced commanders, such as Alexander Gorbaty-Shuisky, who led the eventual successful assault on the city. Indeed, in his early years he was still willing to listen to the counsel of a select circle of figures, such as his confessor, Father Sylvester, Princes Andrei Kurbsky and Dmitry Kurlyatev-Obolensky and Alexei Adashev, some of whom wanted to see reform of the autocratic Muscovite system. Over time, though, he would become increasingly suspicious of those around him: Kurbsky eventually defected to Lithuania; Adashev and Sylvester fell from favour; and Dmitry Kurlyatev-Obolensky was eventually forced to become a monk, and later strangled. Ivan's later reign was a time of fear, violence and suspicion.

Contemporary accounts agree that he was tall and well-built, long of nose and with a piercing gaze. Even as a teenager, he affected a thick, reddish beard. Educated and articulate, he grew to command his surroundings, with the German ambassador Daniel Prinz, who visited Ivan later in his reign, noting his 'large, narrow eyes that observe everything most carefully'. The traveller Jacob Reitenfels concurred on his physique, but added that 'he never laughed except in danger and during his atrocities, so that he was in the best of spirits every time he arranged a disgusting massacre of people'.

The commander of the Main Regiment was **Prince Alexander Gorbaty-Shuisky**, a scion of one branch of the mighty boyar Shuisky family. An experienced voivode as well as military commander, in 1546–47 he led forces from Nizhny Novgorod as part of a campaign along the Volga which acted as a prelude to Ivan's first campaign. He would become governor of Kazan after its fall, a mark of the faith Ivan had in him, despite a brief period in disgrace in 1545. Like so many boyars, though, he would eventually become a victim of the tsar's deepening paranoia, and was executed with his son in 1565, bringing an end to the line of Gorbaty-Shuisky.

Later, **Prince Andrei Mikhailovich Kurbsky** would become one of Ivan's most outspoken critics, after he defected to Lithuania in 1564 at the height of the Livonian War, where he would not only enter into a spirited and angry correspondence with the tsar, but also write a critical memoir-history. At this time, though, the energetic Kurbsky was one of Ivan's closest and most trusted allies, and despite suffering serious wounds to the head, shoulders and arms while driving out Crimean invaders on the eve of the invasion of Kazan, he would still play a key role in the siege and subsequent battle, commanding the Right-Hand Regiment.

The deputy commander of the Main Regiment at Kazan, **Prince Mikhail Vorotynsky** was one of the outstanding commanders of his time. He was of high boyar birth, able to trace his lineage back to the Ryurik dynasty, which founded the early cities of the Rus', with sizeable holdings in what is now Kaluga Region. Although his wealth and birth – and the degree of autonomy it granted him – meant that he was always the subject of suspicious rumours, with claims at times that he might defect to either the Lithuanians or the Crimeans, he remained close to Ivan and would play a key role in successive campaigns against Kazan. He commanded the Right-Hand Regiment during Ivan's 1547 campaign, and the Left-Hand in 1549. He had replaced Mikulinsky at Sviyazhsk by 1552, charged with overseeing the assembly of materials, food and ammunition for the attack. Unusually for a 'fighting boyar', Vorotynsky seems to have understood the importance not just of tactics and individual martial prowess, but also of logistics.

At a time when military engineering was essentially regarded as a necessary but menial task, fit for foreigners and commoners, **Ivan Grigorievich Vyrodkov** was a trailblazer as the first such specialist to become known to posterity by name. He came from the *pomeshchik* class,

Ivan Vyrodkov was unusual in his skill and interest in military construction. Here, he is supervising the construction of new walls for the city of Galich. For all his value to Moscow, he would fall foul of the murderous paranoia of Ivan's later reign, being murdered by his *oprichniki*, his private army-cum-political police. (Facial Chronicle [Illustrated Chronicle of Ivan the Terrible], public domain, via Wikimedia Commons)

his family having long served the Muscovite princes, and worked within the Razriadny Prikaz, literally the Discharge Office, but in effect the monarch's ministry of war. He was unfashionably fascinated with the mechanics of warfare and construction, and was the man behind the pre-fabricated assembly of Sviyazhsk fortress. In the capture of Kazan, he was the deputy commander of the Artillery Regiment, but was primarily responsible for the siege works.

In many ways, **Shigalei's** career exemplified the fluid loyalties of the age, and the degree to which even the dividing lines between Christian and Muslim polities were less sharply drawn than many assume. Son of Shigavleyar, khan of the Qasim Khanate, a vassal state of Moscow's, he succeeded his father to the throne on his death in 1516. In 1519, though, thanks to Muscovite pressure, he was invited to become khan of Kazan, but he was overthrown in 1521, especially because the Muscovite emissary, Fyodor Karpov, insisted on trying to intervene in the khanate's internal affairs and treating Khan Shigalei as if he were a subordinate. Shigalei subsequently served in Muscovy's service, becoming a favourite of Vasily III's until 1533 when, just before the grand prince's death, he was accused of treason and exiled to Beloözero, only being released in 1536 by Yelena Glinskaya, the future Ivan IV's mother and regent, and returned to the Qasim throne. He led contingents in support of successive Muscovite wars with Kazan, and in 1546 again briefly assumed its throne, before being expelled by Crimea's Safa Giray, an experience he repeated in 1551–52. He would later play a key role as a Russian general in the Livonian War.

KAZAN

The ambitious son of Khan Kasim of Astrakhan, **Ediger-Magmet** was more of an adventurer than a committed champion of the khanates. In 1542, he had taken up service with Muscovy, and in 1550 had even taken part in Ivan's second campaign against Kazan, before leaving Russian service and instead joining the Nogai. Seeing him as a useful potential figurehead, in 1551 conspirators contemplated calling on him to replace Shigalei, hoping this would ensure his candidacy had the support of both the Astrakhan and Nogai Khanates. This plan came to nothing when Shigalei rounded up the plotters, but after he had fled the next year, Chapkyn Otuchev, the Kazan statesman and political fixer who was heading an interim government, invited him to become khan. Ediger-Magmet accepted, but prudently brought with himself a detachment of Nogais, aware of how quickly a khan could lose the support of the city's mob or dignitaries. He always had an eye for the main chance, though, and would in due course surrender when Muscovite forces stormed Kazan and enter Ivan's service. In 1553, he was baptized as

The Tatars raided widely, from the Near East to Lithuania, and left their cultural mark, including the 'Lajkonik March' in the Polish city of Krakow, celebrating their survival after being sacked by the Mongol-Tatars in 1241. (Dominika Zarzycka/NurPhoto via Getty Images)

Simeon Kasayevich, married a Russian noblewoman and was granted the city of Zvenigorod.

A senior figure within the Kazan elite, **Chapkyn Otuchev** was more statesman than general. He took part in the initial negotiations around Shigalei's potential submission to Muscovy, but was sufficiently alarmed by the danger of simply becoming a possession of the tsar that he played a key role in barring the city to Mikulinsky and the choice of Ediger-Magmet as the new khan. He would fall early during the battle for Kazan, no warrior, but enough of a patriot to be willing to take his place in the front line.

The dominant imam (religious leader) in Kazan at the time of the siege, **Kul Sharif** was a *sayid*, the green-turbaned descendants of the Prophet Muhammad, who had lived previously in both the Crimean and Astrakhan Khanates. A poet, astronomer and preacher, he was asked to take part in the negotiations with Moscow in 1551 precisely because of his reputation with the wider population and his suspicion of the Russians (and pro-Crimean feeling). The hope was that if he underwrote any agreement, then it would be more legitimate at home. As it was, he proved an intransigent delegate. When war came, he mustered a unit from amongst his own followers, and at the end, was killed on the roof of his own mosque, his body cast down to the cobbles. He would later become a Tatar national hero, and a new Kul Sharif Mosque was built in 1996–2005 inside the walls of the Kazan Kremlin.

A *murza*, or hereditary prince of Kazan, **Yapanchi** was a prince of the nearby vassal-city of Archa and a dashing cavalry commander. He and his brother Shabolat were still mustering forces at Archa when the Russians laid

As a focus for resistance against the Muscovite seizure of Kazan, Ivan ordered the original Kul Sharif Mosque symbolically destroyed, but after the collapse of the Soviet Union it was equally symbolically rebuilt. (© Mark Galeotti)

siege to Kazan, so he led his cavalry squadrons in hit-and-run attacks on the enemy supply lines that were so successful that Gorbaty-Shuisky himself led an expedition against Archa that forced Yapanchi to give battle lest he lose his own base of operations. Yapanchi was killed in the engagement, but the remnants of his force would then play a significant role in the subsequent guerrilla war against the Russians.

The mythic Atalyk

The History of Kazan purports to be a factual chronicle compiled by a Russian who lived as a prisoner in the city for 20 years, but it contains much that seems wholly fanciful, including reference to a mighty Tatar warrior, known as Atalyk, oddly enough also the name of one of the city's gates. He is presented as a superhuman fighter, who 'would ride, angry, upon a hundred daring fighters, and throw all the Russian regiments into confusion, and, having killed many, ride away; those whom he overtook and caught up with, he would cut in two with his sword from head to saddle, for neither helmet nor armour could protect from his sword. And he would shoot at a target more than a mile away, and from that distance he would kill birds, and beasts, and men. In stature and bulk, he was like a giant, his eyes bloodshot, like those of a beast or a man-eater, and … every man was afraid of him'. Nonetheless, surprised and in his cups, Atalyk was reportedly surrounded and finally killed by spear-wielding Russians. A dramatic story of this 'praiseworthy commander of Kazan', but probably entirely fictional.

OPPOSING FORCES

> The Kazanians rushed to meet the Russian regiments,
> And with a cry they began a bloody massacre,
> Like wolves, they burst into the midst of our forces,
> Bloody streams instantly flowed,
> Russian warriors are divided,
> They could not be quickly united into regiments;
> From one side, a cloud of arrows flew like hail;
> On the other side, death roared, the fire of muskets burned.
> – *Rossiyada*

While his first two campaigns against Kazan had been failures (although, according to the sycophantic *Kazan Chronicle*, this was because the Tatars 'overcame him not by their strength, but by their cunning and military slyness'), it was a mark of Ivan's capacities as ruler and commander in those early days that he learnt their lessons well. It was not simply that he realized how unpredictable weather could make traditional approaches unfeasible, but he realized he would need not just new tactics, but different kinds of forces to deliver the kind of decisive blow for which he was looking. To this end, he needed to elevate commanders of demonstrable competence, not just high birth. He would need infantry better trained and equipped than the traditional militias, and not just fighters but engineers, logisticians and other specialists, even if he had to hire them from abroad. In this, he was stealing a march on Kazan. No one doubted the Tatars' courage and determination to defend their city. Some Russians scholars later suggested

Four metres in length, *Blessed Be the Host of the King of Heaven* is one of the largest icons ever painted, and represents the capture of Kazan. It shows Ivan following the Archangel Michael on his return from a conquered and burning Kazan, he and his army feted by angels. (Fine Art Images/Heritage Images/Getty Images)

that they had perhaps become complacent after Ivan's earlier reversals, not appreciating the extent they were more due to the weather than their own efforts. However, it was more the case that the Kazan elites had for years been consumed with internecine political wrangles. There had been little serious thought given to how best to defend the city and the khanate, and it was still relying on the same forces that it had deployed in the past, which were better suited to the enslave-and-loot raid than a siege.

MUSCOVY

The early half of Ivan IV's reign was a time of genuine state-building, and many of the institutions of the modern Russian state chart their ancestry back to the structures that he established, from the Ministry of Internal Affairs to the Ministry of Foreign Affairs (which look back to the Banditry and Ambassadors' Offices, respectively). This also applies to the military: Russia's traditional dependence on artillery and the very notion of a standing infantry army were really Ivan's bequests to the nation. He had, after all, inherited a military structure that suited neither his military needs nor his political interests, one based around militia cavalry raised from and by the gentry, and led by boyars and their personal retinues. This was still an essentially feudal organization, and left the monarch dependent on the nobility and their willingness to muster when he called. It was also a force that originally emerged above all to combat mounted nomad raids, when mobility and elan were crucial. Commanders were generally selected in order of seniority through *mestnichestvo*, roughly translated as 'placeism' (see box), and tended to be more eager to demonstrate their bravery (and seize

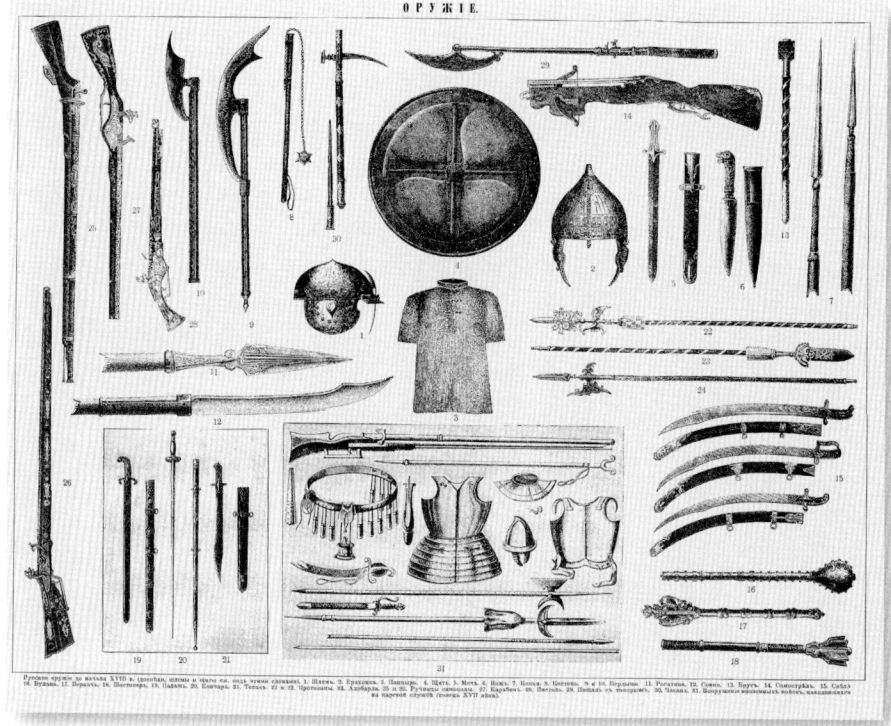

A compendium of typical Russian weapons and armour of the time. The crossbow was very much in decline, being replaced by the arquebus, but note the continuing use of mail (soon to become obsolete in the gunpowder age) as well as the broad-bladed *rogatina* (mid-left), an evolution of the boar spear, and at the top right, an unwieldy arquebus-halberd hybrid. (*Brockhaus and Efron Encyclopedic Dictionary*, public domain, via Wikimedia Commons)

Mestnichestvo

The feudal foundations of the Muscovite army were best illustrated by the practice of *mestnichestvo*, which got its name from the word for place, *mesto*. Intended originally to create a coherent and transparent chain of command at a time when each army was a bespoke collection of levies raised from a changing collection of local princes and potentates, it was in effect a hierarchy drawn up by the Razriadny Prikaz. The order derived from each nobleman's lineage, service and territories. Voivodes would be assigned positions in strict order of their place on the list. Of course, the problem was that this seniority did not necessarily reflect ability, or even how well individuals cooperated or had particular skills matching the needs of any specific campaign. Obviously, a grand prince or tsar could bend the rules, but overall it constrained his allocation of command responsibilities. Not even Ivan could simply ignore it, though. He did everything he could to dissuade aristocrats from challenging the chain of command on the basis of *mestnichestvo*, though, from banning such petitions while on campaign in 1550, to making it clear that he would look unkindly on those who stood on precedence. As a result, he only had to adjudicate on a couple of such cases a year, on average. The system would eventually be abolished in 1682.

valuable loot) than discipline. The infantry was looked down upon, an array of urban regiments, peasant levies and mercenaries, while the still-crude but developing artillery was often the preserve of foreign specialists. In other words, this was still a force shaped by aristocratic privilege and prejudice, geared for the kinds of wars Muscovy no longer needed to fight, and Ivan would prove determined to change all that.[1]

The total size of the Muscovite host is a heavily debated issue, not least as contemporary chroniclers – which estimated it up to an utterly implausible 150,000, according to the *Kazan Chronicle* – tended substantially to overrate the numbers involved. In practice, it would have been difficult to raise and field many more than 30,000–40,000 men, although it is possible that non-combatant labourers, camp followers and hangers-on might have brought the total to 70,000 at the absolute most. As was traditional,

---

1 See Men-at-Arms 427, *Armies of Ivan the Terrible: Russian Troops 1505–1700*

This illustration of Ivan IV entering Kazan is fanciful in that it actually took place in the midst of battle, but does give a good sense of the typical accoutrements of Muscovite aristocratic cavalry at the time, including the conical helmets, with or without the nasal guard. (Universal History Archive/Universal Images Group via Getty Images)

the Muscovite army was divided into six or seven regiments (*polki*) of wildly varying sizes, in most cases from a few hundred to a few thousand. These were divided into smaller units called a *sotnia*, or 'hundred', which would, indeed, generally be of around a hundred men under a *sotnik*. Each *polk* was led by two or more voivodes, under whom would be a small staff of clerks and messengers and subordinate commanders known as 'heads' (*golovy*). Each regiment had its own specific role in the battle and place on the line.

The *Peredovoi Polk* or **Advance Regiment** would take up a position ahead of the main line of battle as skirmishers and a screen against the enemy's own. They would generally be light cavalry, armed with both sabres and composite bows, in a manner very similar to their Tatar foes. In the invasion of Kazan, this appears to have been around 6,000 strong under Alexei Basmanov, a lesser boyar later to become one of Ivan's right-hand men and enforcers. A reconnaissance force known as the **Yertaul** would be raised from the Advance Regiment, typically of several hundreds of light cavalry, selected both for their mobility and their experience, as they would often be first into the fight and also the unit best able to capitalize on an enemy rout. The Yertaul in this campaign comprised around 1,000 of the regiment's men, under Prince Pyotr Shuisky, who was the deputy commander of the *polk* as a whole.

The **Main, Right-Hand** and **Left-Hand Regiments** (*Bolshoi, Pravoi Ruki* and *Lyevoi Ruki*, respectively) would form the bulk of the battleline. The Main Regiment was typically the largest formation, made up of both heavy cavalry and infantry, and was intended to deliver the decisive blow, while the smaller Right- and Left-Hand Regiments guarded its flanks, although they might also be flung directly into the battle if a tactical opportunity presented itself. In the invasion of Kazan, the Main Regiment (commanded first by Mikhail Vorotynsky then Prince Gorbaty-Shuisky) numbered around 10,000, the Right-Hand Regiment (commanded by Pyotr Shchenyatev and

A detail of a map drawn up by German diplomat Sigismund von Herberstein shows what he calls 'fighting serfs', but which, by their relatively basic armour and weapons, are presumably the retinues of *pomeshchiki* or possibly *dyeti boyarskiye*. (Sigismund von Herberstein, public domain, via Wikimedia Commons)

Alexander Gorbaty-Shuisky) 6,000 and, as was customary, Yuri Bulgakov's Left-Hand Regiment was much smaller, with some 3,000 men.

The **Guard Regiment** (*Storozhevoi Polk*) was the rearguard, an all-cavalry force that would also screen the slower-moving supply train and artillery on the march or in battle, and which could be used in a move of desperation as a reserve. Commanded by Prince Vasily Serebryany-Obolensky, it was notionally around 5,000 strong, although in practice it was probably closer to 3,000 as many of its horsemen were instead attached to the Sovereign's Regiment.

If the army was being led or accompanied by the tsar, then it would also contain a specially formed **Sovereign's Regiment**, under his notional command, although in practice the responsibility of Prince Yuri Pronsky-Shemyakin, one of Ivan's closest aides. Typically drawn exclusively from gentry and boyar cavalry deemed especially loyal or in royal favour, its role was to defend the tsar or follow him to glory in battle at a decisive moment, depending on the monarch's character and inclination. During the invasion, it was around 3,000 strong.

Then there would also be an **Artillery Regiment**, which comprised both heavy guns and also units armed with the primitive light cannon known as the *tyufyak*. As Ivan began to raise his own standing force of *Streltsy* armed with arquebuses, though, increasingly the Artillery Regiment would exclusively deploy cannon, as the infantry were increasingly equipped with firearms. The regiment was commanded by Pyotr Morozov, with Ivan Vyrodkov as his deputy and chief engineer.

The aristocratic cavalry

The traditional heart of a Russian army, even if it was already beginning to be supplanted by the infantry, was cavalry, armed and trained to fight much more like nomad horsemen from the east (even if they rarely could match the Tatars' skills in horsemanship) rather than the post-feudal cavalry of Europe. These forces were still recruited on the basis of class and service to

As demonstrated by this Russian re-enactor, Russian cavalry were sufficiently heavily armoured for the melee, but also had come to learn the importance of horse archery and mobility from the Mongol-Tatar armies. (OLGA MALTSEVA/AFP via Getty Images)

the sovereign. Even the hereditary aristocrats, the *dvoriane*, held their estates by the grace of the tsar, but the lesser service gentry, the *pomeshchiki*, were even more directly bound to the needs of the state. They received their lands, the *pomestiya*, with the direct understanding that this was to allow them to maintain themselves and their retainers, ready for war, and were only held so long as they were willing and able to serve.

Along with the *dyeti boyarskiye* – literally 'children of the boyars', but really an intermediary rank between boyars and service gentry – they made up the bulk of the cavalry. Some could be considered heavy cavalry, typically boyars and their retainers, who could afford such expensive items as mail-and-plate armour and heavier horses (although nothing like the massive warhorses of western European feudal chivalry). The majority were more lightly armed and armoured, usually in a quilted jacket called a *tegilyai*, but, either way, they were almost all able to both skirmish and fight in the melee, being armed with bows, as well as spears and hand-to-hand weapons. The bows were eastern-style composite ones of laminated horn and wood, relatively compact and carried in a case on the left of the saddle, with a quiver of iron-tipped arrows to the right. They would typically also bear a long-shafted spear (or sometimes a *rogatina* boar spear with a larger head and crossbar), as well as sabre or mace.

Each *pomeshchik* was expected to be able to muster fully armed and armoured, and with two horses, with extra retainers, similarly equipped, if his *pomestiye* holdings were larger than the minimum. The expectations of the *dyeti boyarskiye* were similar, while boyars would often be able to field larger contingents, outfitted at their expense. Instead of relying simply on a well-padded quilted leather or linen caftan, perhaps under a light mail shirt or a *zertsalo*, a circular metal plate strapped over the midsection, these successors to the *druzhina*, or personal retinue of medieval lords, would often wear heavier coats of mail or scale, or a *pantsir*, a mail-and-plate cuirass. Even the lowliest cavalryman would seek to ensure he had a simple conical helmet, with more elaborate designs in use by the more wealthy. After all, this was an era of display, and cavalry would wear bright, even gaudy colours and if they could accessorize their weapons, panoply and armour with gold, jewels and other inlays, they would. English traveller Anthony Jenkinson wrote of the Russian cavalryman:

Armed with swords, axes, maces and bows, most of the infantry in the Muscovite army were relatively ramshackle feudal levies, although in many cases they had been on multiple campaigns and thus were relatively battle hardened. (PHAS/Universal Images Group via Getty Images)

> When he rides on horseback to the wars or on any journey, he has a sword of the Turkish fashion and his bow and arrows of the same manner. They use saddles made of wood and sinews with the tree gilded with damask work and the seat covered with cloth, sometimes of gold and the rest saffian leather, well stitched.

The Streltsy and other infantry

The traditional emphasis on the aristocratic cavalry left the infantry as a rag-tag collection of low-prestige units, including the so-called *pososhnye lyudi*. These 'assembled people' were militias raised from the villages at a ratio of one man from each three, five, ten or thirty households, depending on the scale of the need. In times of peace, they were essentially impressed labour, used for construction, clearing canals and moats and similar manual labour. On campaign, they were likewise often used for digging ditches, building fortifications and dragging siege guns into place, but would also be expected to fight, albeit typically with at best a quilted fabric or leather jacket and a spear, axe or bow. Aged between 25 and 40 years, they were meant to be in good health, capable archers, who also knew how to ski. In practice, their quality varied greatly. Some joined enthusiastically, hoping for a chance for plunder, while in other cases the levy was seen by the village elders as a good opportunity to turf out the infirm, unruly or unproductive.

However, the Gunpowder Revolution was beginning to make itself known, even in Muscovy, and the European way of war was increasingly relying on a core standing army that was ever more a foot rather than cavalry force. Russian infantry in the past could often be doughty in battle, but were essentially regarded as an adjunct to the horse, and made up of a heterogenous collection of levies and mercenaries raised whenever needed. Although the first hand-held gunpowder weapons in Russia date back to the end of the 14th century, having been imported from Germany, by the beginning of Ivan's reign, units of archers and close-combat infantry were supplemented by contingents of *pishchalniki* armed with the *pishchal*, a clumsy arquebus or matchlock musket. Some were mounted and armed with matchlock pistols, although they fought on foot; the rest were infantry. In 1545, for example, the conquered city of Novgorod was required to raise 2,000 *pishchalniki* for a campaign against Kazan, evenly divided between foot and mounted troops. However, they, like other Muscovite infantry, were just temporary levies, raised for a campaign then returning to civilian life.

As a result, in 1550, Ivan made the first moves towards establishing his own standing army, creating the first *Streltsy*. The name literally means 'Shooters' but is perhaps best translated as 'Musketeers' because while at this stage not all of them actually were armed with the *pishchal*, this was

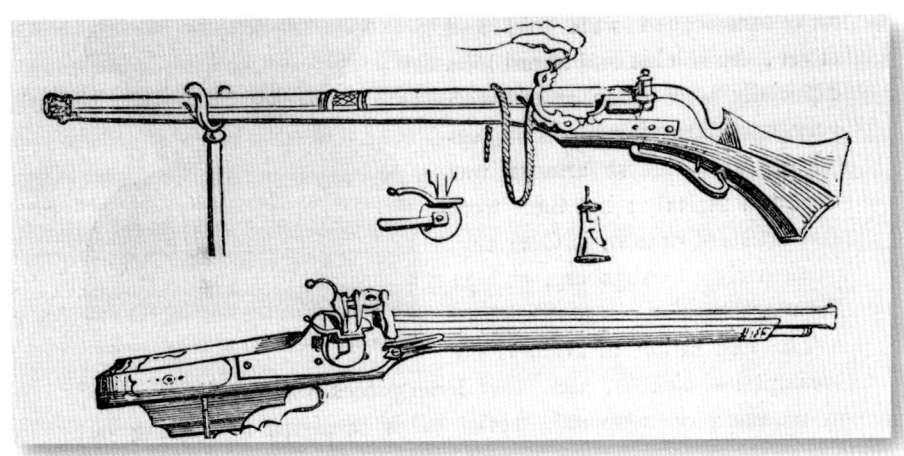

The matchlock *pishchal* of the mid-16th century was a heavy and clumsy weapon, yet nonetheless it would soon replace first the crossbow and then even the composite bow. (Bettmann/Getty Images)

It would be decades before the *Streltsy* were quite as disciplined and uniform as this representation by Sergei Ivanov, but it does convey just how unusual it was for Moscow finally to field a standing army rather than a ramshackle collection of feudal levies equipped any which way. (Fine Art Images/Heritage Images/Getty Images)

to be one of their signature weapons, along with the *berdysh*. This was a short, crescent-bladed poleaxe that would also be used as a rest for the heavy arquebus. Initially, Ivan raised some 3,000 of them, in six battalions of 500 men each, further subdivided into hundreds. Recruited for life, they were granted smallholdings in Moscow's Zamoskvorechiye neighbourhood, rations of rye, oats and salt, and an annual salary of up to seven rubles, comparable to a *pomeshchik* cavalryman, as well as the right to engage in small-scale business, such as artisanal handicrafts, while not on campaign. In time, they would expand to a much more sizeable force, but it would be at Kazan that they would first be able to demonstrate their value. Unlike the rest of the levy infantry, in which each soldier might have different armour, clothing and equipment, the *Streltsy* wore a common uniform and were trained and equipped to match. Each *Strelets* wore a heavy kaftan and coat in the same colour as the rest of his battalion, a tall, fur-lined hat, a sabre, *berdysh* and, for about two-thirds of them at this time, a *pishchal*.

Cossacks and Tatars

Muscovy also made extensive use of forces raised from vassal states as well as mercenaries and temporary allies. Many, ironically enough, were Tatars, including Shigalei, there for the kill, along with a handful of his followers who had also been driven from Kazan. Indeed, the contemporary Tatar writer and philosopher Rafis Salimzhanov has claimed – perhaps hyperbolically – that during this campaign, more Tatars fought for Moscow than Kazan. Some were mercenaries, but most were 'Service Tatars' from communities that had sworn their allegiance to the tsar, such as the Qasim Khanate. They provided both infantry and cavalry, under their own commanders, which would then be attached to one of the regiments. Indeed, Tatar cavalry were much prized for the Sentry Regiment. A similar approach was taken with other vassal communities, such as those 'Hill Mari' (Mountain Cheremis) living along the left bank of the Volga River who had swapped allegiances back and forth, and some remained under Russian influence, providing some infantry for Ivan's host, even as other Mari fought for Kazan. There were also Mordvins from Temnikov, another vassal region technically under the authority of the Qasim.

Another significant source of troops were the Cossacks. Settlers who migrated into the 'Wild Fields' in what is now southern Ukraine, between Muscovy, Poland and the Kazan, Nogai and Crimean Khanates, formed fiercely independent communities of hunter-farmers, their skills honed by resistance to periodic Tatar slave raids. In due course they would largely divide between the Zaporizhian and Don Cossack Siches (as their confederations were known), the former looking west, the latter north-east, but at this time they were still relatively divided and autonomous. Moscow's princes – and later tsars – would offer payments and land in return for military service, often simply to rely on them as guardians of the southern borders, but also as a further source of light cavalry in time of war.

Guns and engineers

The first Russian firearms dated back to the 14th century, including a primitive bombard for siege warfare and a smaller cannon known as the *tyufyak*, which fired what the Russians called *drob*, handfuls of stones and metal offcuts. These were ungainly, and often of limited effectiveness once enemies were no longer scared by their noise and smoke, but with the establishment of the first cannon foundries in the late 15th century, notably the Pushechny Dvor, or Cannon Yard, inside the Moscow Kremlin, largely set up by Italian and other foreign specialists, Russian guns became both more reliable and deadly, and portable. The *tyufyak* would become smaller and more portable until the next century, when it was fully replaced by hand-held weapons such as the *pishchal* and more capable cannon. Meanwhile the Russians had cumbersome heavy cast-bronze siege guns, able by the mid-16th century to throw a cannonball weighing up to 40lb a distance of a little more than a mile on a very good day, although their effective range was less than half that. Each of which had its own name, such as Nightingale, Ushataya and Flying Serpent. The Russians were also beginning to acquire early field artillery, so-called 'little cannon' to the 'big cannon' of the siege guns. The range of the latter guns were closer to 0.3 miles, but like their larger brethren, they could fire solid shot of stone or iron weighing up to 18lb.

Traditionally, the artillerymen, the *pushkari*, were drawn from the urban population and commanded by relatively educated lesser *pomeshchiki*, as this was a low-status occupation.

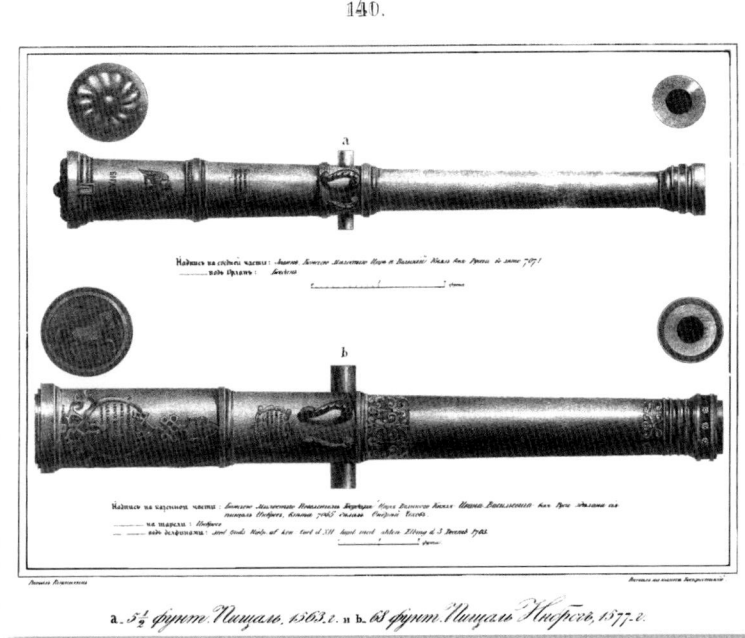

A 5.5lb gun and a massive 68lb cannon, measured by weight of shot. The Russian artillery of the day was becoming increasingly capable. English ambassador Giles Fletcher observed that 'none of the Christian rulers has such good artillery and such a supply of shells as the Russian Tsar'. (Public domain via Wikimedia Commons)

The broad class of *sluzhilye lyudi* or 'service people' included not just *dyeti boyarskiye* and *Streltsy*, but a range of other free subjects nonetheless required to serve in times of war. Sergei Ivanov's *Inspection of the Service People* shows the process whereby local levies were raised, both soldiers and *pososhnye lyudi* auxiliaries. (Historic Images/Alamy)

There were also numerous foreign mercenaries, although Ivan would make a concerted effort to develop a suitable cadre of Russian engineers, gunners and gunsmiths. In due course, Ivan would recruit a standing force of artillerymen who, like the *Streltsy*, were paid a salary and rations of flour and salt, while being allowed to earn money on the side trading or as artisans, when not on campaign.

Engineering had likewise been regarded as a 'German profession' – the Russian word *Nemtsy*, German, being used as a catch-all for all Europeans – who would boss over collections of craftsmen such as carpenters and blacksmiths, and large contingents of *pososhnye lyudi* labourers. Again, this would begin to change through Ivan's reign, but was still very much the case at Kazan. There, a crucial role was played by Ivan's chief engineer, considered to be a master of subterranean mines and explosives, known as 'Butler', whose contested identity is discussed later.

Logistics

As far as possible, the army would forage on the march, but even when regiments travelled by different routes so that they all drew on fresh lands, it was rarely possible to meet more than a fraction of its needs this way. Each soldier was also expected to bring their own rations, including dried meat or fish, buckwheat to make *kasha* porridge and the hard, twisted ring loaves known as kalaches or *sukhar*, portions of dried rye bread. Beyond that, though, the army travelled with extensive supply train with food, forage, ammunition and gunpowder, managed by the *poshoshnye lyudi* and replenished at towns along the way, carried in wagons, sleds or river boats, as the season and route dictated.

KAZAN

> I fear the Tatars most of all. They are as fast as the wind upon their enemies, for when they march they cover five or six days' road in one day, and when they run away they disappear as quickly. Especially important is the fact that their horses do not require shoes, nails or fodder. When they come to a river they do not wait for a boat like our troops. Their food, like their bodies, is nothing much; their strength is shown by the fact that they do not care for comfort.

This was the appraisal of Selim I the Great, Ottoman Sultan until 1520 and a man who, ironically, had relied on Crimean Tatars to supplement his forces in his wars of imperial expansion. Even by the 16th century, after all, the Tatar way of war still relied heavily on its traditional strengths of ferocity, speed, mobility and coordination, using cavalry in the classic steppe nomad manner. Operations were conducted with as much secrecy as possible, often launched on moonless nights and involving the deliberate sowing of confusion and disinformation.

The Tatar way of war

Although increasingly living in cities and towns rather than roaming the steppe, the Tatars of Kazan and the other khanates retained much of their old style of warfighting, one built around the raid. A raiding army might well set out along one clearly defined route of march only to make a sharp turn towards another objective, while sending out parties on diversionary attacks to confuse the enemy as to their strategic intent. These *chambuls*, detached raiding parties, would move with a speed that would befuddle the armies of their more sedentary foes and contributed to the panic – *trwogi tatarskie* or

The Tatar way of war was very much an evolution of that practised by the Mongols, as they swept across Eurasia. (Barry Lewis/In Pictures Ltd/Corbis via Getty Images)

'Tatar frights' to the Poles – which would help disrupt their enemies' defences further. One chronicle's account of a raid by Kazan Tatars in the 1540s, for example, noted that 'the people fled to the advancing [Russian] host, and they jammed the bridge and ran heedlessly through the soldiers' lines, and so overcome were they with pity for their Christian brethren' – or, more likely, put in disarray by the influx of refugees – 'that they put off their advance until the morrow, by which time the ungodly devils had already withdrawn, taking with them plunder and slaves'.

Speed was of the essence, and Isaac Massa, a Dutch grain trader and envoy to Moscow, provides a compelling account of this:

> As soon as the Muscovites became aware of the enemy's flight, they sped large detachments of cavalry in hot pursuit to prevent him from burning everything in his path. Arriving in Serpukhov, they learned that the Tatars had already crossed the Oka [River] that day. This seemed incredible to them. They could scarcely believe that such a vast army could, in one night and half a day, and in summer, make a march of 28 miles, and cross a great river.
>
> Yet so it was, for the enemy were endowed with inconceivable speed in flight, as in war they encumber themselves with neither munitions nor victuals. The Tatars, who feed on horseflesh usually take two mounts for every man on their expeditions. When one of the two is tired, the rider jumps on the other, and the first follows his master like a dog, as these horses have been trained to do while very young.

A Tatar army would be assembled on the basis of a muster of able-bodied men above the age of 15, in Kazan's case typically through the *begs* or governors of each of the ten separate territories in which the khanate was divided, as well as from the khan's own personal fiefdom, known as the Bulgar vilayet. Under usual circumstances, there would often be a degree of discretion – men might well be eager to serve for the chance of booty or glory, while others might have a compelling reason to stay home. The local *beg* might also want to limit or maximize the size of the force he raised, in some cases

This Turkish re-enactor displays armour and helmet typical to high-status Turkic warriors of the age, from Constantinople to Kazan. Note the sabre, elaborately decorated conical helmet and the reinforced mail. (MUSTAFA OZER/AFP via Getty Images)

to protect the local economy (and thus his tax base), in others because of particular support for or opposition to the khan of the day. Nonetheless, the underlying understanding was that in a time of true crisis, a khan could demand a comprehensive mobilization. In 1501, for example, Crimean Khan Mengli Giray announced:

> I want to mount my horse and you must be all ready to fight alongside me. There must be one cart for five men, three horses to a man … [and] a great quantity of arms and food. No one is to stay home save he who is less than fifteen years old. Whoever stays behind is no servant of mine, of my sons, nor my princes. Rob and kill such a man.

Given that it was impossible to mobilize the entire male population, especially when defending their own lands, women and children were often brought into the army. There are accounts of boys as young as 12 serving as auxiliaries, herding horses, carrying water, capturing spoils and working in the camp, while learning the arts of war from their fathers and older relatives. Indeed, for the siege of Tavan in 1697, the Crimean khan would mobilize boys as young as ten or 11. The khans of Kazan were slightly less prone to such practices, but even so from records there were certainly teenagers participating not just in the final defence of the city, but also in the efforts to hold back the Muscovite advance. However, the fact that when 15-year-old boys were captured, their age was specifically indicated in the Russian records, something not done for adult men, suggests that they were a relative rarity and curiosity. Based solely on these records, no more than 3–5 per cent of Kazan's front-line fighters were below the age of 17. Women were not forcibly mobilized to fight by any of the khanates (although, again, they often would fight in the last-ditch defence of their homes, as happened in Kazan). When they were conscripted, again, it was as a source of labour behind the lines. Nonetheless, there were a few cases of women actively choosing to

Like the Mongols before them, the Tatars were masters of the false retreat, drawing over-confident enemies into traps. In this miniature from the *Scylitzes Chronicle*, Bulgar Tatar cavalry are withdrawing during the siege of Thessaloniki, precisely to encourage the Byzantine forces to leave the security of their walls. (Werner Forman/Universal Images Group/Getty Images)

fight, although the lack of any references to such in the Muscovite accounts of this war – until it came to the storming of the city – suggests not in this instance. The *Rossiyada*, admittedly, talks of one of Kazan's heroes being 'a fearless girl, bold as a fierce boar, ferocious as a lioness', but there seems no historical basis for this claim.

In battle, the Tatars would use hails of arrows and surprise and flank attacks to disrupt enemy formations and pre-empt their own plans, while scattering in the face of attacks by their often more heavily armoured enemies. False retreats intended to draw the attacker into a disadvantageous position were common, as was the rapid regrouping and counterattack once the enemy formation had lost its discipline and cohesion in the charge. However, Kazan's forces, while still predominantly structured for the offensive, had been influenced by the need to resist sizeable Muscovite attacks over the years, as well as the growing role of the Ottoman empire in Tatar politics. Both of these influences led to a growing importance for both infantry and artillery, but while Kazan had begun to adopt simple handguns, their artillery was still inadequate in number and antiquated in design.

Kazan's transition

After all, Kazan's forces were, arguably more than any other khanates', in the early stages of a transition away from their Golden Horde roots. They had begun to be organized in a distinctive manner reflecting both that nomadic tradition and the realities of a more settled, semi-sedentary state that had to stage raids both to take slaves and also to retain the strategic initiative, but which also needed to face the threat of a more numerous and advanced Muscovy.

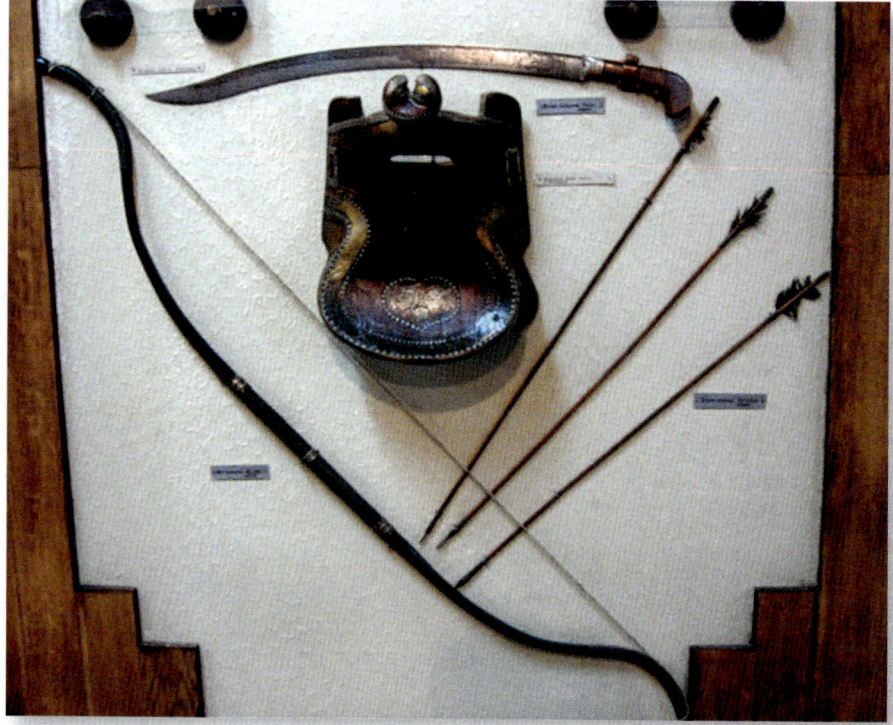

A display of classic Tatar arms and armour from the Ternopil Museum of Local History, including the classic sabre called an 'Ordynka' or 'Horde' sabre by the Russians, given its origins in the weapons borne by the invading Mongols. (ru:User:Russianname, CC BY-SA 3.0 https://creativecommons.org/licenses/by-sa/3.0, via Wikimedia Commons)

These poor-quality miniatures are nonetheless amongst the very few near-contemporary illustrations we have of soldiers specifically from Kazan. To a great degree, they look like those of any other khanate, however the central and left-hand figures show some Russian cultural influences, especially in their hats and headgear, reflecting the cultural influences that followed the increasing sedentarization of the Tatars. (Adam Olearius, public domain, via Wikimedia Commons)

In theory, Kazan's forces retained the Mongols' original decimal structure: ten men to a squad generally called an *arban*, ten *arbans* forming a 100-man *jaghun*, a squadron or company, and ten of them comprising a *guran*, or regiment. They never truly organized up to the 10,000-strong *tumans* the Golden Horde would field, though: the formation size existed, but more as an administrative than field unit. In practice, their organization was mission-specific. On a raiding campaign, an army's *gurans* would likely be broken or grouped into *chambuls*, whose size could range from several hundred to a few thousand men. These, in turn, would comprise a number of *torhaks*, of anything from ten to fifty men, which was the smallest unit which might operate independently. In the defence of Kazan, though, the defenders were formed into *gurans* generally known by either the name of their commander or where they were recruited, and assigned either to one of the gates (with responsibility also for the adjacent stretches of wall) or else the khan's own reserve.[2]

Although again some Russian chroniclers wilfully over-estimate the size of the defending force at up to 70,000 – which the city and its food supplies would not have been able to accommodate – their total strength was likely closer to some 30,000 of their own troops, of whom at least two-thirds were cavalry, along with 2,700 Nogai cavalry originally brought by Khan Ediger-Magmet when he took the crown, augmented by a relative handful of more recent arrivals. There were also small numbers of other allies and mercenaries, but the overall tally was around 35,000 at the very most.

Cavalry

Despite a degree of cultural influence from neighbouring states and peoples, the forces of the Kazan Khanate were still largely equipped like their nomadic forebears. High-status cavalry would wear lamellar armour

---

2 See Men-at-Arms 491, *Armies of the Volga Bulgars & Khanate of Kazan, 9th–16th Centuries*

(and in some cases even their horses were armoured), and they, like their Russian counterparts, would be armed with spears as well as bows and hand weapons. These were relatively few in number, though, largely confined to the guards of the palace and the retinues of the most powerful local princes.

Most, though, were much more lightly equipped, and relied on speed and agility more than armour. They wore the characteristic *chapan*, a heavy sheepskin jacket that could be worn fleece out in summer, inwards in winter, over which they might wear a leather jerkin or mail hauberk. Either way, most were horse archers, equipped with a powerful compound bow and a sabre. Some also bore spears, but this was unusually in addition to, rather than as an alternative to the bow. Their skill as archers was legendary, and they typically had a range of some 350m, and could fire accurately out to 100m.

Infantry
While raiding armies were often all cavalry in the interests of mobility, the Tatars also deployed infantry, especially in the defence. Even more so than for the Russians, though, this was a low-prestige service, typically a local levy. Some wore long mail shirts, metal breastplates and conical helmets, and carried small round shields and spears or sabres. Most, though, were archers, unarmoured or simply in padded coats, or in some cases musketeers. Although the Tatars began using firearms relatively early, they fell behind in their development, and were still largely using very primitive and inaccurate guns that were little more than a short iron pipe attached to a wooden rail, although in the defence of the city some did also use slightly more advanced 'hook-guns'. These were heavier weapons intended to be rested on a parapet, with a hook that would be placed on the other side of it to absorb the punishing recoil.

Many civilians would also fight in the climactic final storming of the city, driven by fear of what would follow, Muslim piety or simple patriotism. They were generally unarmoured, and armed with whatever they could find to hand, from bows and swords picked up from the bodies of fallen defenders, to simple clubs, knives and cleavers. Nonetheless, in the tight confines of the city, sheer numbers and desperation could often count against even better-armed, trained and disciplined enemies.

The city's defences
Although the Tatar style of war tended to place the emphasis on the rapid, highly mobile raid or attack, in this conflict they were on the defence and thus could rely on the fortifications of Kazan itself, as well as its population. The city was well-fortified, surrounded by a double wall made of oak beams filled with rubble and clay silt, atop a 3–4m-high earth bank. At its thickest, along the Kazanka River, this was 6m broad. The walls were topped by a wooden-roofed walkway and firestep. Around the wall were 14 stone towers, made of large limestone blocks, roughly dressed and bound together by limestone mortar. The preserved height is some 4m, including ten rectangular gatehouses of varying size and strength. To the north was the Kazanka River, while on the other sides was a dry moat that at its widest stretched some 7m. The Bulak River flowed through the western half of the city, and where the Bulak met the Kazanka north of the walls the ground was swampy to the point of near-impassability.

Kazan, 1552

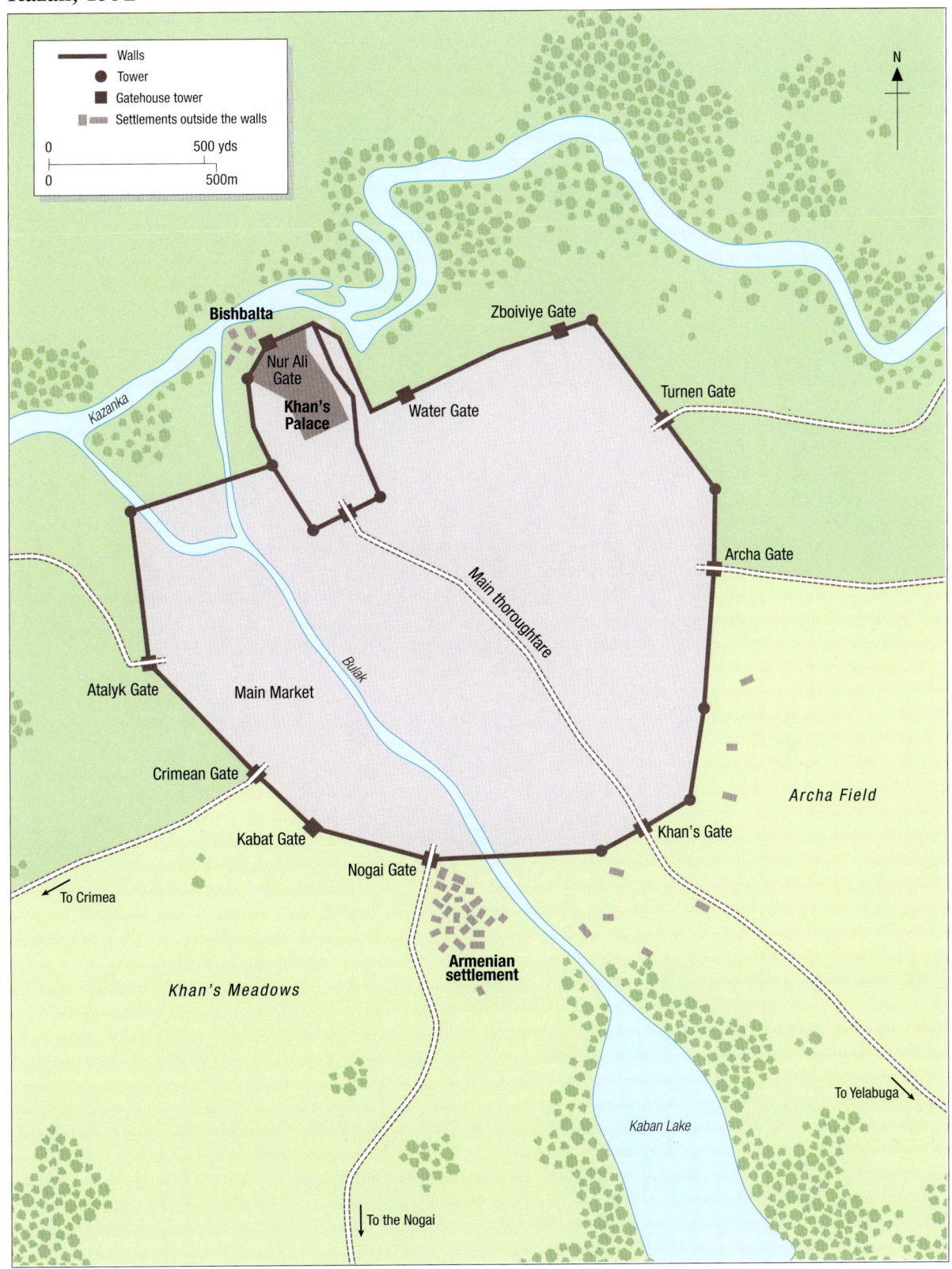

The gates of Kazan

The city's gates were crucial to any attempts to take the city. Whereas in the siege of 1548, according to the accounts of a contemporary, one Haji Serefi, the people of Kazan only really had actively to defend six gates, including the Khan's Gate, in 1552 all ten faced a greater or lesser threat. Clockwise from the northernmost, they were:

1. Nur Ali Gate: As one of the few gates leading directly into the Khan's Palace precincts, this was relatively heavily fortified, and equipped with a number of cannon.
2. Water Gate: The Yeibuga (Water) Gate was so named because beneath it was a channel bringing fresh water from the Kazanka.
3. Zboiviye Gate: Although by no means accounted the strongest of Kazan's gates, this portal resisted attempts to batter it open and was instead opened from the inside after the Russians were already within the walls.
4. Turnen Gate: Eventually, this gate was not breached so much as bypassed when the adjacent walls were brought down by an underground mine.
5. Archa Gate: The gate leading onto Archa Field was the largest and best defended of them all, and would prove to be central to the siege and the storming of the city.
6. Khan's Gate: The most splendid gate, connected directly by the city's central thoroughfare to the Khan's Palace.
7. Nogai Gate: The road towards the Nogai Khanate was important for trade, as well as the frequent political contacts with this political chameleon of a state.
8. Kabat Gate: Quite why this was known as the 'Level Gate' is something archaeologists and chroniclers alike have failed to confirm.
9. Crimean Gate: While named for its position on the main route ultimately leading to Crimea, the presence just inside of the main market also earned it the nickname of the 'Merchants' Gate'. Its wide gate, suited to carts of produce, would be breached and stormed by the Left-Hand Regiment in the final assault.
10. Atalyk Gate: Opening as it did to a path along the Kazanka River, this was largely used by fishermen.

Inside the city, granaries and other warehouses were well-stocked with provisions, and a series of wells provided ample fresh water, and the calculation was that they could outlast any siege, especially so long as the Bulak River was undammed. The walls of the Khan's Palace were not quite as high as the city's outer ramparts, but in the main they were made of good quality oak logs, and were partly faced by a protective ditch, although in many cases, wooden warehouses, shops and homes were built right up to them. The walls were still in the process of being replaced with a stone rampart, and some of the towers and gatehouses were stone, too.

There were some admittedly smaller and simple cannon mounted on some of the stone gatehouses, including the Archa, Khan's and Crimean Gates. They were often things of beauty, intricately and extravagantly cast

This reconstruction at the Old Kazan Reserve in Vysokogorsky District, Tatarstan, gives a good sense of the style of Kazan's walls, even though the gatehouses – but not the intervening towers – were of limestone, albeit with the same wooden roofs. (Obsrevatoria, CC BY-SA 4.0 https://creativecommons.org/licenses/by-sa/4.0, via Wikimedia Commons)

and engraved, but as field weapons they were substantially inferior to the Russians', typically with a calibre of around 3–5in, and prone to misfires and even spontaneous explosion. There seem to have been no such guns mounted on the walls or towers of the khan's citadel other than the Nur Ali Gate.

Tatar allies

Despite Ivan's conclusion of a – strictly temporary – peace with the Nogai Khanate, Ediger-Magmet's close connection with the Nogai ensured that, thanks to his status and promises of generous payment, he could also count on a contingent of some 2,700 cavalry, drawn from ulus, or clans, from the right bank of the Volga, under a *murza* called Zaynash.

Beyond that, his main allies were drawn from the Mountain Cheremis. As with so many other peoples of the region, to the Cheremis, alliances with Moscow or the khanates were simply ways of surviving and prosecuting local feuds, and they would often play one power off against the other. In 1546, Prince Tugai of the Mountain Cheremis swore allegiance to Ivan in return for troops to assert his authority over the rest of his people and the Meadow Cheremis on the other bank. However, the construction of Sviyazhsk on their ancestral territories caused growing friction, and although Ivan offered gifts and tax exemptions, he made it clear that Muscovite power was there to stay, and he expected the Cheremis also to supply troops for his campaigns against Kazan. In effect, he was treating at least the Mountain lands as not being a vassal state, but annexed. As a result, many of the Mountain Cheremis threw their lot in with Kazan. Before the invasion, they occasionally harassed Sviyazhsk, but during the war, they would become more active and determined in their attacks on the Russian rear. These numbered perhaps 1,000 skirmishers, archers and javelin men, who were no match for the Russians in the melee, but who would prove a disproportionate nuisance in the earlier stages of the siege, as they used their woodcraft to conduct raids on the Russians from the woods north of Kazan.

For centuries, the nomadic horse tribes from the east – Bulgars, Pechenegs, Mongols, then Tatars – had shaped the nature of war on the steppe, dominated by the kind of fluid cavalry skirmish shown in this 10th-century manuscript. Arguably Kazan's mistake was to maintain its own cavalry forces, and seek more from the Nogai, rather than to appreciate the rising role of gunpowder and infantry. (Photo 12/Universal Images Group via Getty Images)

OPPOSING PLANS

> Having defeated the Crimeans, we will also overthrow Kazan;
> We will destroy the villainous plans of the Horde,
> Let us go and destroy their first hope.
> I myself, I myself am going against these Tatars.
> – *Rossiyada*

Although he undoubtedly appreciated the political advantages in great shows of piety, Ivan was also deeply religious, and his planning for the invasion included prayer and consultations with Sylvester and other senior clergy. (© Fine Art Images/Heritage Images/TopFoto)

MUSCOVY

The invasion

Ivan first ordered the resumption of an on-off blockade of Kazan's river traffic in late 1551, but while many of his court assumed he would again launch a winter campaign, the tsar had suffered too much from the vagaries of the weather and now had a forward base at Sviyazhsk to which supplies could be delivered by river and stockpiled. He spent more time than before drawing up plans and, above all, gathering everything that his campaign would need. By the end of March, barges began heading along the Volga from Nizhny Novgorod to Sviyazhsk, bearing supplies, ammunition and the first of the siege guns Ivan planned to use to break Kazan. With them went Princes Alexander Gorbaty-Shuisky and Pyotr Shuisky, charged with making preparations for the invasion: first, clearing the forests between Sviyazhsk and Kazan from Tatar forces and then preventing any reinforcement of the city, not least by ravaging its hinterland. When he arrived, Ivan instructed Gorbaty-Shuisky and Serebryany-Obolensky 'to burn the Kazan lands and villages, destroying them to the ground', detaching a substantial cavalry force from the Main Regiment to this mission.

Meanwhile, in May–June, Ivan was mustering his army. The Right-Hand Regiment formed at Kashira, but Ivan made the symbolic decision that the main gathering would be at Kolomna, where in 1380 Moscow's Grand Prince Dmitry Donskoi had assembled his army before heading off to defeat the Golden Horde at Kulikovo.[3] To draw even more heavily on his mythologized ancestor's example, Ivan even brought with him Donskoi's own war banner, under which the Sovereign's Regiment would march and fight. There also assembled the Main, Left-Hand and Advance Regiments, while the Yertaul and the Guard Regiment gathered at Murom. Contingents then took separate routes towards the theatre of operations so as to prevent over-foraging and undue bottlenecks on the way: even so, a column could stretch far, with the pathfinders five days ahead of the rearguard.

The Crimean Tatar incursion towards Tula meant that the bulk of the Advance Regiment had diverted south to beat it off, before it, the Main and Right-Hand Regiments took a southern route towards Kazan, via Ryazan. Meanwhile, the Sovereign's and Sentry Regiments, with Ivan at their head, marched first for Vladimir, where they joined the Left-Hand Regiment, and then for Murom, where they were met by allied Tatar troops under Shigalei. They were mainly from the Qasim Khanate but also included two princes from the Astrakhan Khanate, who had fallen foul of local politics. They headed to meet the rest of the army on the banks of the Sura River. The various elements were gathered together on 4 August and then set off for Sviyazhsk, where they were also joined by supplies and the Artillery Regiment, which had travelled down the Volga. From Sviyazhsk, the combined force moved on to Kazan.

The plan, such as it was, could be characterized as deceptively and brutally simple: to surround, besiege and seize Kazan, making it for once and for all a subject of the tsar.

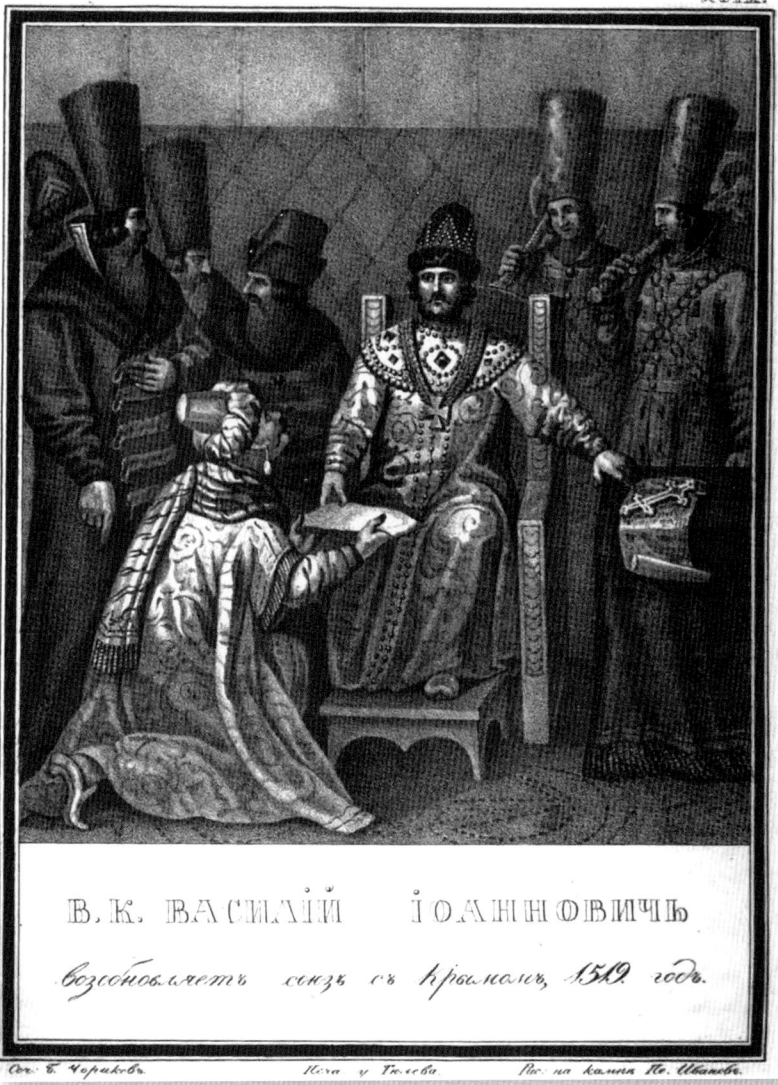

The Crimean Khanate had a long record of tense relations with Muscovy. Here, Vasily III, Ivan's father, receives an ambassador from Crimea, after he has been forced to pay tribute following Tatar victories in battle. (Fine Art Images/Heritage Images/Getty Images)

---

3   See Campaign 332, *Kulikovo 1380: The battle that made Russia*

THE MARCH, JUNE–AUGUST 1552

Ivan's army was drawn from contingents across Muscovy, and featured both cavalry elements (which would largely travel overland) and infantry and artillery (best moved by river). The result was a complex exercise in command and logistical coordination, even without the complication of needing to repel a Crimean Khanate attack on Tula.

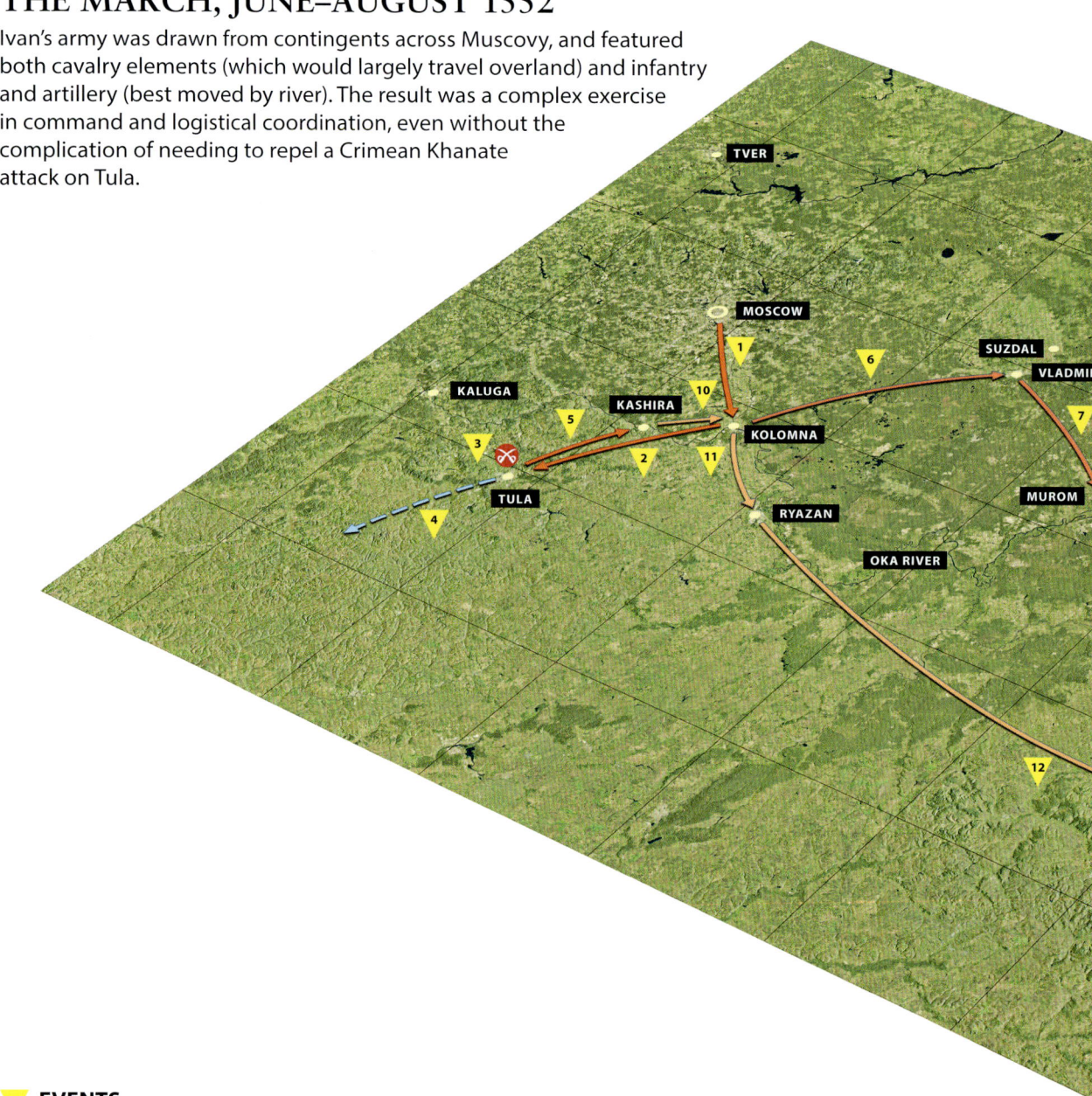

▼ EVENTS

The initial muster and defence of Tula

1. Ivan musters at Kolomna (16 June)
2. Relief force sent to Tula
3. Siege of Tula lifted (24 June)
4. Crimean forces retreat
5. Advance Regiment returns to Kashira

Ivan's march

6. Ivan, at the head of the Sovereign and Sentry Regiments, marches to Vladimir
7. Reinforced by the Left-Hand Regiment, they march on to Murom
8. Joined by Tatar allies at Murom
9. They head to Alatyr to join the rest of the army

The Main Regiment's march

10. The Advance Regiment rejoins the host at Kolomna
11. The Advance, Right-Hand and Main Regiments march to Ryazan
12. They head to Alatyr to join the rest of the army

The final march

13. The Artillery Regiment heads to Sviyazhsk along the Volga
14. The army crosses the Sura River and heads to Sviyazhsk (4 August)
15. The fully united army crosses the Volga and besieges Kazan (23 August)

Note: gridlines are shown at intervals of 100km (62.1 miles).

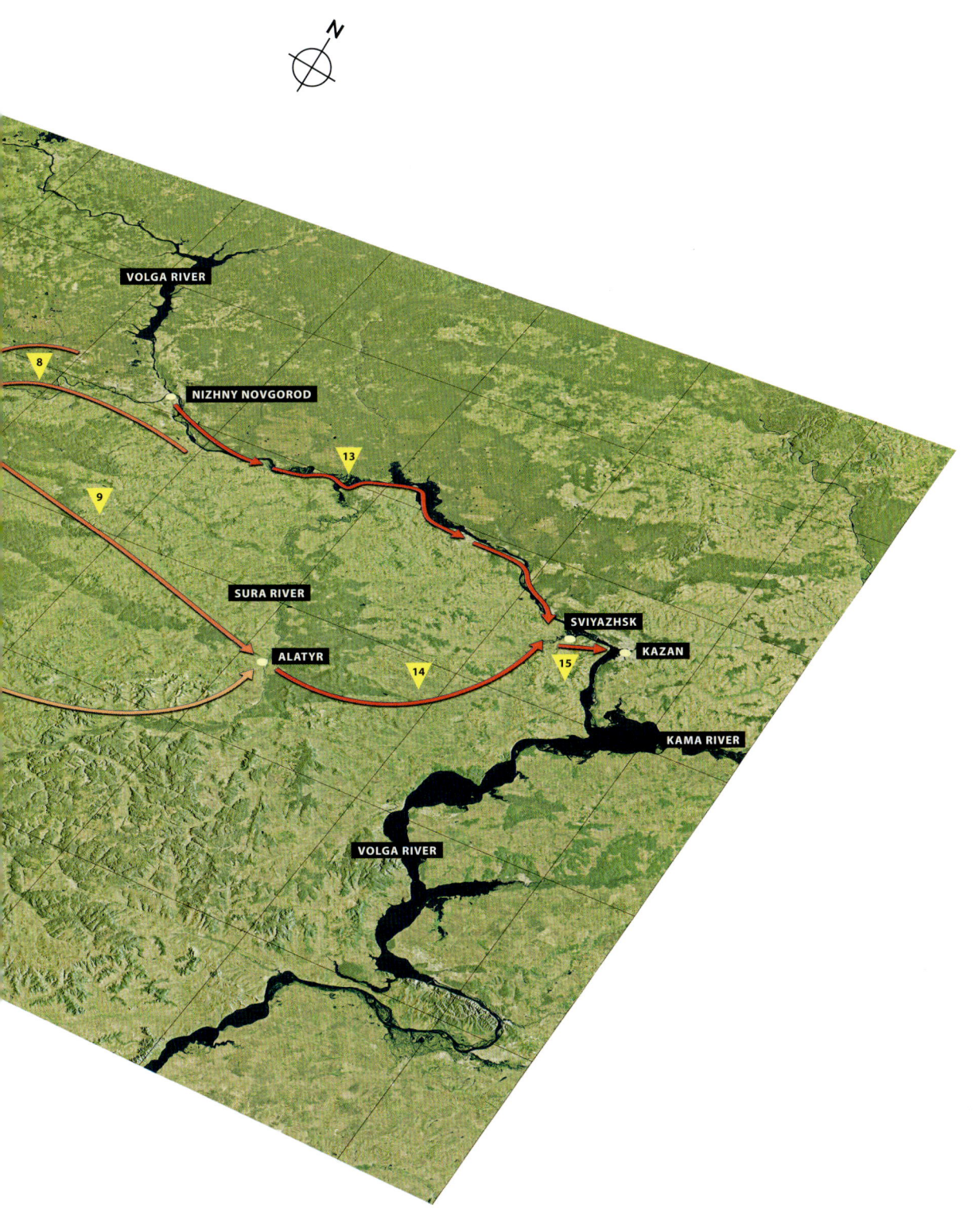

KAZAN

The defence

Kazan's options were much more limited than the Russians'. First of all, once it became clear that Ivan was preparing for another attack, Khan Ediger-Magmet sent out emissaries in the hope of gathering allies. This proved disappointing. He had brought some 500 of his supporters from the Nogai when he had taken the throne, and sought to encourage Khan Yosuf to help defend Kazan, either by sending warriors or staging – even just threatening – an attack into the undefended Muscovite heartlands in the hope of diverting Ivan. However, the best Yosuf was willing to offer was to turn a blind eye to any of his men willing to follow Ediger-Magmet. Having supported Moscow against Kazan in 1548, then broken with Ivan, Yosuf was unwilling to incur the tsar's wrath further. While Ediger-Magmet's personal connections and reputation (as well as the opportunity to have a scrap with the Russians) did persuade more than 2,000 Nogai to come to Kazan, largely drawn from the unruly ulus living along the right bank of the Volga, this would be the sum total of any assistance from that quarter. Likewise, the Crimeans, after their defeat on the Shivoron River, were in no mood again to exert themselves on Kazan's behalf.

As Tatarstan today begins to get back in touch with its Islamic roots and khanate past, there has been an effort to rehabilitate Ediger-Magmet, although this is difficult given the lack of surviving images of the man and the importance of the incorporation of Kazan into Muscovy for the modern multi-ethnic Russian Federation. (Connect Images via Getty Images)

Some accounts suggest Kazan's defenders also included a contingent of warriors from the Siberian Khanate to the east. Given how quickly its leaders Yadgar and Bekbulat congratulated Ivan on his conquest of Kazan and subsequently began paying Moscow a small but symbolically important tribute, it seems more likely these were mercenaries rather than any kind of official support, and they likely numbered no more than a couple of hundred. Beyond that, there were also a smattering of other foreign fighters, from Crimeans to a small levy raised from the inhabitants of the Armenian

Siberian warriors

The northernmost successor state to the Golden Horde, east of the Ural Mountains, the Siberian Khanate was ethnically more varied than the others, with Urals peoples such as the Ostyaks and Voguls (today known as Khanty and Mansi) in their number, as well as Siberian Tatars. This meant that the khanate was more of a fractious confederation and put sharp limits on the authority of the khan. Thus, while co-rulers Yadgar and Bekbulat were anxious not to alienate Moscow (ultimately a fruitless mission, with the khanate essentially defeated by Cossacks under Yermak Timofeyevich in 1582), they were unable to prevent warriors joining Kazan's cause, out of a mix of sympathy and mercenary zeal. They were markedly behind the times, even compared to Kazan's forces, without firearms and wearing old-fashioned chain or lamellar armour. Nonetheless, even amongst the Tatars they were famed for their accuracy with the composite bow, and their hardiness on the field.

village, most of whom were merchants and their retinues.

The next step was to prepare the city for a siege. It had adequate supplies of fresh water and food was brought in from the surrounding villages. Contingents of troops were also recalled from outlying settlements, although as these were often the retinues of local magnates, they did not always comply, preferring to protect their own interests. In other cases, they were unable to muster their forces and reach Kazan soon enough to slip past the Russian siege. This was the case with Princes Yapanchi and Shabolat of Archa, and so, true to the Tatar way of warfare, they were instead charged, along with the Cheremis skirmishers, with hounding the Russian supply lines and attacking their rear.

Although there was some hope that the Russians might be halted on the banks of the Volga, or forced to withdraw if weather or daring raids destroyed their stocks of food or gunpowder, in practice Kazan expected this time to face a siege. But the mood seems to have been one of hopeful resignation: they would have to hunker down behind their walls and prepare, hoping to outlast Ivan's patience and supplies. After all, they had done it before, and so it was reasonable to hope that they could do it again. Reasonable, but mistaken.

A Nogai warrior. Despite the frequent political contacts between the Nogai and both the other khanates and Moscow, this Nogai shows far less of the cultural influence of either, including the armour favoured by his cousins from Kazan. (Adam, Jean Victor, 1801–67, public domain, via Wikimedia Commons)

The Siberian Khanate would not escape the Muscovite expansion. Here, Kuchum Khan and his men would face their final defeat in 1598. (Fine Art Images/Heritage Images via Getty Images)

THE CAMPAIGN

> The Russian regiments are burning with vengeance,
> They merged with the Kazan ones, like two rivers,
> Where the waves form a stormy current,
> They push each other back, they suppress each other,
> The warriors huddled together in the rising dust;
> – *Rossiyada*

At first, the omens seemed troubling for the Russians, and some feared this, the largest expedition yet against Kazan, would be as unsuccessful as the previous ones. That spring, plague erupted in Sviyazhsk. Meadow Cheremis from the right bank of the Volga, supported by Chuvash from the east, rebelled against Moscow, and Semyon Mikulinsky was forced to lead a column of troops to suppress the rising. And, of course, the Crimean Tatars would soon strike at Ryazan and then Tula. Nonetheless, by the end of June, the plague had subsided, Mikulinsky had defeated the scattered rebels in detail, and the Crimeans had been forced to retreat.

All seemed clear, and on 3 July Ivan himself set out from Moscow for Kolomna. On 15 August, his forces crossed the Volga on specially made barges. Khan Ediger-Magmet hoped to repel the invaders at this point, when they were at their most vulnerable, and mustered perhaps 10,000 soldiers, to meet the Russians on the river's banks. The march had indeed been tough for many of the Muscovite troops (and their horses). Prince Kurbsky recounted the overland journey as 'about five weeks of hunger and dire distress'. Many soldiers died or dropped out on the way because of a lack of drinking water and abnormally high temperatures. However, when the overland troops met the 'ship army' that had come down the Volga, they had been able to replenish themselves ('we had our fill

The *Tatars Dance*, by Yulish Kossak, illustrates a high-speed clash between Tatar and Cossack. The goal of Ivan's strategy against Kazan was to lock down the city and sweep away forces outside the city, so the defenders could not use their advantage in mobility against the slower-moving Muscovites. (Tibbut Archive/Alamy)

Quite why the Russians disembarked earlier and approached Kazan by land instead of attacking across the Volga becomes clear once one sees just how wide the river is at this point: this is a view of Kazan from the far bank, before reaching the Kazanka. (Petar Milošević at sr.wikipedia, CC BY-SA 3.0 https://creativecommons.org/licenses/by-sa/3.0, via Wikimedia Commons)

of dry bread with much relish and thanksgiving … [for] we had had none for about nine days') and briefly rest before moving on. As a result, they were not in quite as weakened and demoralized a state as Ediger-Magmet had hoped. More to the point, the Yertaul had already been ferried across by the time the Tatars arrived and, with the help of other troops from the Advance Regiment who were disembarking literally as battle was joined, the scouts managed to hold enough of a bridgehead for more and more troops to be able to cross the river. After a bloody battle lasting three hours, the balance of power shifted. Having originally been severely outnumbered, barge by barge the advanced Muscovite force was sufficiently reinforced that it was able to push the Tatars back. Ediger-Magmet opted to accept defeat and preserve his forces for the inevitable siege, withdrawing in good order, something the exhausted Russians were in no state to prevent. Ivan issued a *pro forma* demand for Kazan's surrender; the khan equally formally refused.

The next day, Kamai Khuseinov, a *murza* from Kazan, defected to the Russians, bearing intelligence about both the composition of the Tatar forces and the state of the city's defences. Vorotynsky and Vyrodkov, the most interested in the intricacies of siegecraft of all of Ivan's generals, eagerly pounced on the latter and with their engineers began to plan how best to break the city's walls. Meanwhile, Alexander Gorbaty-Shuisky and Pyotr Shuisky – voivode of the Yertaul – led a force of elite light cavalry drawn from the Advance Regiment out to scour Tatar communities and scouting parties from the woods as far as the Kazanka River, north-east of Kazan.

Tatar cavalry were feared for their mobility and ferocity, and this image shows their characteristic bows, quilted armour (akin to that of many of the Russians) and hardy mounts. (DE AGOSTINI PICTURE LIBRARY/Getty Images)

The way was soon clear. On 23 August 1552, the first Muscovite forces reached the Archa Field southeast of Kazan, and the siege would truly begin shortly thereafter.

ARCHA AND KAMA

A particular concern for the Muscovites, given the Tatars' strategic mobility and delight in the flank and rear attack, was the danger posed to their supply lines, artillery park and ammunition stores by raiders from outlying settlements. They were right to be so given that Prince Yapanchi of Archa (Arsk, to the Russians) and his brother Shabolat were still at liberty. Having been unable to gather their forces in time to make it to Kazan before the Russians closed their lines around the capital, they were instead charged by Ediger-Magmet with doing all they could to undermine the siege.

The Battle of Archa (Arsk) Field, 1506

In 1505, another war between Kazan and Muscovy erupted after Khan Mohammad Amin seized the goods of Russian merchants attending the fair in the city and then launched abortive raids in alliance with the Nogais against Murom and Nizhny Novgorod. Ivan III began to prepare retribution, but then died, his son Vasily III succeeding him. This delayed Moscow's response until May 1506. One army, under Prince Fyodor Belsky, advanced along the Volga, while another, under Prince Vasily Kholmsky, one of Ivan III's sons-in-law, took a land route. Belsky failed to coordinate his advance with Kholmsky and his army was taken in the rear by a large Tatar cavalry force under Khan Amin himself, and all but routed. However, soon after, Kholmsky's force engaged with Amin's at Archa Field and defeated them, forcing them to withdraw into the town itself. The Tatars had been rich with booty taken from Belsky's army and their raiding of settlements on the way, and the Russians fell to looting. This gave Amin the opportunity to sally from the town and attack while the Russians were distracted, dispersed and disorganized, delivering a devastating defeat on them. It was a triumph, but Amin had come to appreciate that he had been lucky this time, as Muscovy could raise new armies and come at him again, and so opted to sue for peace. Vasily III, more concerned with Lithuania, was happy to agree. Nonetheless, the Battle of Archa Field in June 1506 would remain a powerful symbol of Kazan's capacity to challenge and defeat Muscovy.

This was a mission that suited Yapanchi's aggressive spirit and his light cavalry forces: he had at least 2,000 cavalry, and beyond his personal squadron of heavier horse, most were nimble, lightly armed horse archers, ideal for hit-and-run raids. So successful was he in interdicting Muscovite supply caravans that the invading army was soon put on restricted rations, something that immediately damaged morale and worried Ivan. Furthermore, the Tatars began coordinating sorties from Kazan with Yapanchi's attacks, signalling to him with flags from the walls.

However, Yapanchi's strength, his independent base at Archa, was also his vulnerability. Unable to close with the Tatar forces, Gorbaty-Shuisky led a mixed force of horse and infantry against Archa. Yapanchi was as temperamentally unsuited to allowing his base to be taken as he was aware that it would force him to withdraw towards the Kama River to the south, from whence it would be much harder to maintain the tempo of attacks. Besides, ever since the 1506 Battle of Archa Field, when a Tatar defeat at the hands of the Russians was turned into a crushing victory at the eleventh hour, the Russians had learned the dangers of complacency: they did not only have to ensure they bottled up the defenders in Kazan, they also needed to be sure there were not sizeable raiding parties at their back.

At the centre of Archa was a wooden fortress deemed one of the Tatars' strongest, but Yapanchi knew that it, and the city's low wooden walls, would not be able to resist the handful of siege guns that were being hauled up to join Gorbaty-Shuisky's force. He characteristically opted for a bold strike, taking the initiative in the hope of routing the Russians before their artillery could arrive. The Russian commander had, however, the measure of his enemy. While he led an infantry-heavy force towards Archa along the floodplain of the Kazanka River, he placed a substantial cavalry force under Prince Pyotr Serebryany in woodlands to the north. When Yapanchi launched a cavalry charge on 24 August, the infantry, largely a mix of *Streltsy* and Temnikov

Muscovite light cavalry – Russians and Cossacks – scour the Kazan countryside for remaining Tatar raiders, as well as opportunities for forage and plunder. (Bildagentur-online/Universal Images Group via Getty Images)

Mordvin auxiliaries, remained in close order and met it with a volley of arrows, javelins and arquebus fire. As the Tatars wheeled to respond with their usual storm of arrows, Serebryany's force rode out of the woods, in a move reminiscent of Dmitry Donskoi's victory at Kulikovo, and crashed into their flank. With the river to their left, infantry in front, and heavier cavalry to their right, the Tatars were unable to rely on speed and manoeuvre. Caught in a close-quarter melee, they quickly broke. Prince Yapanchi himself was killed trying to rally his men, and while most escaped, many to fight as guerrillas in the future, for the moment this threat was eliminated. Archa itself quickly fell once the Russian guns had delivered a few demonstrative rounds, stone balls heated in open fires so that they could ignite wooden walls as they smashed into and through them, with 200 Tatar warriors taken as captives. A possibly apocryphal story is that when the prisoners were tied to stakes before Kazan as Ivan urged the city to surrender, promising that if they did the captives would be freed, the defenders feathered them with arrows from the walls, to show their own ruthless determination.

In September, Gorbaty-Shuisky and Serebryany would continue to sweep round the territories east and south-east of Kazan on their campaign to raze further potential bases for resistance and generally to forestall the emergence of other forces able to challenge the Russians. First, they moved on the wooden fortress on the promontory now known as Vysokaya Gora (High Hill), east of Kazan, and left it burning. Then they embarked on a ten-day march through the territories down to the Kama River, destroying a reported 30 'forts' – most of which were little more than stockaded villages – as well as freeing slaves and seizing whatever cattle herds and foodstuffs they could find. These they brought back to the Muscovite lines, to Ivan's evident relief, as his soldiers could eat well again. Prince Gorbaty-Shuisky was rewarded by being put in charge of the Main Regiment.

LAYING SIEGE

While Yapanchi had been raiding behind the Russian lines, the defenders in Kazan had not been idle. The day after his army had arrived before the city, Ivan sent a delegation to make what was presented as a final offer. In return for surrender, the people of Kazan were promised to be able to keep their faith and property as subjects of the tsar, with the khan remaining, but as a vassal of Moscow's. The offer was rejected, and the ambassadors driven from the city to the jeers of the crowd, but Ediger-Magmet planned an even more dramatic expression of defiance. As the invaders were still setting up their siege lines, on 23 August, a major sortie was launched from three of the city's gates simultaneously. According to the chronicles, 15,000 Tatars boiled forth from the city, but in practice it was likely closer to 5,000 – still a serious attack. They chose their ground and moment well, as the Yertaul had only just crossed the Bulak River and were climbing the steep bank beyond, and most of the other Russian troops nearby were still on the other bank. They were saved by the intervention of Cossacks and *Streltsy*, who opened fire at long range with their arquebuses. They did little damage, but attracted the attention of the Kazan troops and had to bear the brunt of their attack. They were pushed back, albeit in relatively good order, but this stalled the Tatar attack. Ivan ordered heavier *dyeti boyarskiye* cavalry from

While most often fighting on horseback, Kazan's defenders did include a substantial number of infantry archers also able to use their bows to great effect against the Muscovites, when they were not under cover. (Sefa Karacan/Anadolu Agency via Getty Images)

the Right-Hand Regiment into the fray, and along with the infantry they were able to push the Tatars back into the city. A crucial role was played by both the *Streltsy* and some of the lighter artillery that had already been brought to the field, and a contemporary account highlights the terrible din 'from the cannon fire and the thunder of arquebuses, and the voices and cries and shouts from both sides and from the clatter of weapons'. The defenders' hopes of being able to break the morale of Ivan's army before it was settled were dashed, but their casualties had been light and they had demonstrated their will and ability to take the battle to the Russians.

The Russians' ability to settle themselves into their siege lines was then further hindered. As they began to dig earthworks and gun pits, they were battered by a rainstorm that turned earth into mud and trenches into puddles. A supply barge was flooded and sank, and then, in what seemed a terrible omen in those superstitious times, high winds blew away the tsar's own tent and the banner of the Guard Regiment. The young Prince Andrei Kurbsky later wrote that the deluge was brought on by Tatar sorcerers, old men and women who shouted out invocations from the city's walls at sunrise. Ivan, himself extremely superstitious, nonetheless exerted himself to show himself amongst his soldiers, and ordered the priests accompanying him to hold a service and reassure the men, holding a procession around the army, bearing what were believed to be fragments of the True Cross to ward off further enchantments. Even so, considering that at this time the soldiers were still on short rations because of Yapanchi's raids, the mood was grim. Ivan himself began to revise his expectations for how long the siege could take and sent dispatches back to Nizhny Novgorod and Moscow ordering the preparation of winter clothes and sleds in case the siege dragged out through the autumn.

THE SIEGE OF KAZAN, SEPTEMBER 1552 (PP. 58–59)

The full range of contemporary siege arts was deployed by the Muscovite force. A siege gun **(1)** batters the walls under the gaze of Ivan himself **(2)**, attended by soldiers bearing his personal flag and the red Banner of the Most Merciful Saviour. Smoke rising from the city demonstrates how the Russians often fired heated shells as incendiaries, although particular targets are the Khan's **(3)** and Archa **(4)** Gates. Meanwhile, *pososhnye lyudi* workers under the cover of woven mantlets **(5)** dig trenches towards the city wall. Others are engaged in the difficult and dangerous task of digging tunnels under the walls **(6)**, which will eventually be stuffed with explosives. Ivan Vyrodkov's imposing siege tower **(7)** mounts both light cannon and *gakovnitsa* heavy arquebuses, to further bring fire on the defenders, and will shortly be moved to face the Archa Gate.

The *gulyai-gorod* 'walking city' was made up of a number of wooden shields mounted on wheels which could be positioned to form various protective bastions on the battlefield. (Belyakovdoj, CC BY-SA 4.0 https://creativecommons.org/licenses/by-sa/4.0, via Wikimedia Commons)

As if this were not bad enough, while Gorbaty-Shuisky and Shuisky's sweeps through the woods around Kazan had largely managed to clear them of Tatar soldiers, the Cheremis woodsmen had largely managed to elude them, in part by falling back, in part by going to ground. In any case, they began harassing the Russians, especially targeting their supply wagons and the *poshoshnye lyudi* labourers who, for all their low status, were crucial to the siege. They would sneak from the woods in warbands of from a dozen to a couple of hundred warriors, often at dawn or dusk, get within range and unleash a volley of javelins and arrows, then withdraw before the Russians could respond. In due course, once the invaders had built a second, contravallation defensive rampart to guard their rear, they were less vulnerable, and parties of Muscovite infantry, especially drawn from their own woodsmen, including from Smolensk and Kaluga, would patrol the near reaches of the forests to pit their skills against the Cheremis. In the interim, thought was even given to the use of the characteristically Russian mobile fortification, the *gulyai-gorod*, but it was decided that given the speed and unpredictability of the Cheremis attacks, this would make little sense.

The *gulyai-gorod*

The *gulyai-gorod* ('walking city') was a rolling fortress of sorts, used by the Russians to provide protective bastions against steppe nomad forces. Instead of being an armoured war wagon such as those used by the Hussites, a *gulyai-gorod* comprised a number of reinforced oaken screens on wheeled frames (or mounted on sleighs in winter). These could be pulled together to form defensive positions in a variety of configurations, from a wall, to semicircle, to a circular enclosure, and reformed as the tactical needs of the moment dictated. They incorporated loopholes for arquebuses and light cannon, and provided useful protection against arrows and primitive handguns. Although they became increasingly anachronistic once the Russians were fighting enemies with cannon, in their debut during the wars against Kazan and then the other khanates, they proved their worth in both defence and attack. Heinrich von Staden, a German mercenary who fought for Ivan, recounted later that 'if the Russians did not have a *gulyai-gorod*, then the Crimean Tsar would have beaten us, taken us prisoner and taken us all away … and the Russian land would have been his land'.

After all, the Muscovites would soon establish their siege lines, to which the *poshoshnye lyudi* would continue to add throughout the campaign. First, trenches were dug right round the walls, other than where the city was flanked by the Kazanka River, where they were dug on the opposite bank. These were backed by low berms of the soil from the trenches, into which were inset positions for cannon, and in due course a second siege line behind this was also built, to protect the besiegers from raids from the surrounding forests. In front of the wider gates in Kazan's walls were then raised palisades to blunt or channel further cavalry sorties. Although the defenders regularly showered the Russian labourers with arrows, they took to working at night or behind shields of woven wicker branches more than 2.5m high – and in any case, Muscovite commanders were perfectly willing to sacrifice labourers' lives to prepare for the next stage of the siege. They also began to dam the Bulak, but they never managed totally to block its flow, especially when it rained.

BY MINE AND CANNON

On 27 August, the Russians were ready, and around midday began to batter Kazan's walls with their artillery. The superiority in Ivan's guns quickly became evident. The Muscovite guns were both more numerous and bigger, able to fire larger cannonballs further. Their accuracy was still mediocre, but even so, the skills of Ivan's newly formed corps of artillerymen proved superior to their enemies'. They began hammering the walls and towers, not least to silence their guns, and also lobbing heated stone balls into the town, setting fires and forcing the population to expose themselves to danger extinguishing them, especially as some projectiles shattered on impact, scouring the area with what was in effect primitive shrapnel.

Meanwhile, Vyrodkov was overseeing the construction of a large wooden siege tower some 13m high and 18m deep. The components were prepared by carpenters to the rear of the army over several days, and were assembled together at night, so that the next morning it seemed to the dismayed defenders that it had magically sprung from nowhere. Its three-storey height meant that it could fire over and down at the defenders on the walls, and it reportedly mounted ten small cannons able to fire a 1lb ball and maybe as many as 50 *gakovnitsy*, which were heavier arquebuses that needed to

The Russian guns and gunners alike markedly outmatched Kazan's, allowing them first to silence the cannon mounted on the city's walls and then batter the fortifications. (Orig. drawing by R. Stein, engraving by P. Dziedzic, public domain, via Wikimedia Commons)

The Muscovites divided their artillery into *bolshoi naryad* and *maly naryad* – 'big cannon' like this siege weapon, and the 'small cannon' which could be used in the field. The former were crucial to the siege of Kazan. (E. Palmquist, public domain, via Wikimedia Commons)

be mounted on a wooden stand. This was wheeled towards the Archa Gate to the east of the city, and soon began to take the Tatar guns defending it out of action.

The Russians were no less active underground. Under the scrutiny of 'Butler', whatever his nationality, workmen were driving a tunnel under the Kazanka River, towards the Water Gate to the north, through which passed the city's main source of fresh water, as the Bulak River was silted, polluted and, by then, partly dammed. On 4 September, 11 barrels of gunpowder were detonated under the gate, blocking the channel and breaching the gate. The mine's success against the gatehouse was greater than expected, and although a hurried assault was launched by the Right-Hand Regiment, which was responsible for Kazan's northern approaches, this proved too little, too late. Few Muscovite troops even reached the damaged gate, being cut down by archers as they tried to cross the river. The city was not without water: there were still other wells and reservoirs, too, and the waters of the Bulak could be boiled. However, it certainly became scarcer, and disease would soon begin to spread.

Spurred on by this success, the Russians began to dig more tunnels, seeking to place more charges under the city wall. The Tatars dug some countermines using dragooned labour from Kazan's citizens, hoping to intercept the encroaching tunnels, but it appears this had little if any effect, not least as they lacked the same numbers of experienced engineers. Realizing that they needed to try and forestall the Muscovites' efforts, on 26 September *oghlan* Aq Muhammad led a dawn attack out of the Archa Gate, hoping to reach and burn Vyrodkov's siege tower. It would prove a valiant but futile

The mysterious 'Butler'

The traditional claim is that the enigmatic Butler was an Englishman, one of many who entered Moscow's service. On the other hand, considering the degree to which Russian military engineering had been dominated by Italians such as Ridolfo 'Aristotele' Fioravanti, the man who, for Ivan III, had built the brick walls of the modernized Moscow Kremlin and the Cannon Yard, and been chief of artillery in campaigns against Novgorod (1477–78), Kazan (1482) and Tver (1485), a spirited case has been made that he was a scion of the Marini family of military engineers. Then there are also the suggestions he was a German known as Herr Asmus, a Dane called Rasmussen, or even a Lithuanian called Erasmus. In any case, at Kazan, this engineer would prove a crucial Muscovite asset through his capacity to manage the digging of tunnels under the city's walls and towers, which could be packed with explosives to breach the defences.

gesture: the Tatar cavalry were unable to make full use of its agility and speed, channelled into killing zones by the trenches and berms built by the Russians, who had not stopped adding to and developing their siege lines. Raked by archers and arquebusiers, they were soon blasted by clouds of *drob*, a primitive precursor to grape shot. They put on a brave show – Prince Ivan Mstislavsky would be gravely wounded by two arrows in the early skirmishes – but when Aq Muhammad's horse was shot from under him, although many of the workers around the siege tower were fleeing, the Tatars quickly appreciated that they were unlikely to be able to take it and they withdrew. Contemporary accounts suggest that they had had little idea of just how dangerous the Russian guns could be at closer range. The defenders even lost control of the half-ruined Archa Gate to the Russian counterattack, although they were unable to push further into the city. Nonetheless, Mikhail Vorotynsky and Alexei Basmanov led several hundreds from the Main and Advance Regiments, respectively, in holding the ruins of the gate for the next couple of days. Another sortie out of the Zboiviye Gate was even less successful, failing to get beyond the Russian siege lines and instead being shattered almost as soon as it left the shelter of the city's wall in a hail of gunfire and *drob*. Accounts speak of the gatehouse being painted red with their blood.

Alexei Basmanov was a hard-fighting general and loyal – some say sycophantic – servant of Ivan's. He was rather less successful as a father, and Alexei (here on the left, being given orders by Ivan on the right) would end up stabbed to death by his son Fyodor (centre). (V. Polyakov, G. Zeifer, CC BY-SA 4.0 https://creativecommons.org/licenses/by-sa/4.0, via Wikimedia Commons)

Many of Ivan's commanders pressed him to order a general assault at this point, not least because, while the defenders were hungry, tired and increasingly subject to disease, the Muscovite forces were beginning to be over-extended and there was concern that the weather might quickly turn wintry. The young tsar hesitated, though. Again, poor weather had delayed the arrival of food and, more to the point, gunpowder. His earlier assaults had failed due to over-confidence and under-supply, and he did not want to repeat the experience. Instead, he stuck to his plan. The siege continued, and with raised gun platforms now having been built facing many of the city's gates, Ivan's cannon could rake both the defences and the city. By night, *pososhnye lyudi* were driving trenches towards the walls and piling earth and brushwood into the defensive ditch. Behind the lines, wooden bridges were being built, ready to be thrown across it in the assault. Ivan was close to being ready.

On 30 September, a mine under the Kazan wall between the Zboiviye and Turnen Gates was detonated, blowing another breach, but it seems as if this may have been a premature blast, or the accidental result of Kazan's counter-mining operations, because again the Muscovites seem to have been unready. Besides, the nearest force was the Yertaul, which was arguably the least appropriate force to clamber over smoking ruins and take the battle to the defenders. Nonetheless, they tried, and were soon reinforced by several hundreds of horse from the Advance Regiment, but this was not enough. (It is possible that Basmanov's absence, still then engaged in the defence of Archa Gate, contributed to the regiment's failure to respond promptly and at scale.) Meanwhile, attacks with scaling ladders were spontaneously launched against the Khan's and Atalyk Gates, with some Russians even making it into the city. This was not enough, however, and after several hours of bitter hand-to-hand melee, the Russians were forced to withdraw to their lines.

The Kazan Crown (in the background) superseded the Cap of Monomakh (foreground) in the tsar's official regalia in 1553, to mark Ivan's victory. It is a rather more ornate item, studded with pearls, garnets and turquoises. (J-F RAFFIN, CC BY-SA 3.0 http://creativecommons.org/licenses/by-sa/3.0/, via Wikimedia Commons)

THE ASSAULT

Ironically enough, the very next day, the new supplies of gunpowder arrived. Ivan again offered the defenders a chance to surrender, to which Ediger-Magmet replied, 'We will not beat our foreheads!' – in other words, bow down in the low kowtow both Tatars and Russians had learned from the Golden Horde – 'There may be Russians on the walls and towers, but we will just build another wall. We will endure or we will all die'. As a result, Ivan decided that there was nothing for it but a general assault, which would be launched at once: 2 October. The evening before, the troops took communion, while in the night, 48 barrels of gunpowder were passed, hand to hand, along the tunnels the Russians had dug under Kazan's gates and walls, largely to the south-east.

Just after dawn, the slow fuses reached the explosives, and the foggy morning was ripped by explosions. The Nogai and Kabat Gates were partially or wholly blown apart, while a wide stretch of the wall between

THE SIEGE, AUGUST–OCTOBER 1552

In under two months, Ivan's forces would finally break Kazan, a testament not only to Muscovy's growing military strength, but also its capacity to sustain a major siege at the end of long and precarious supply lines.

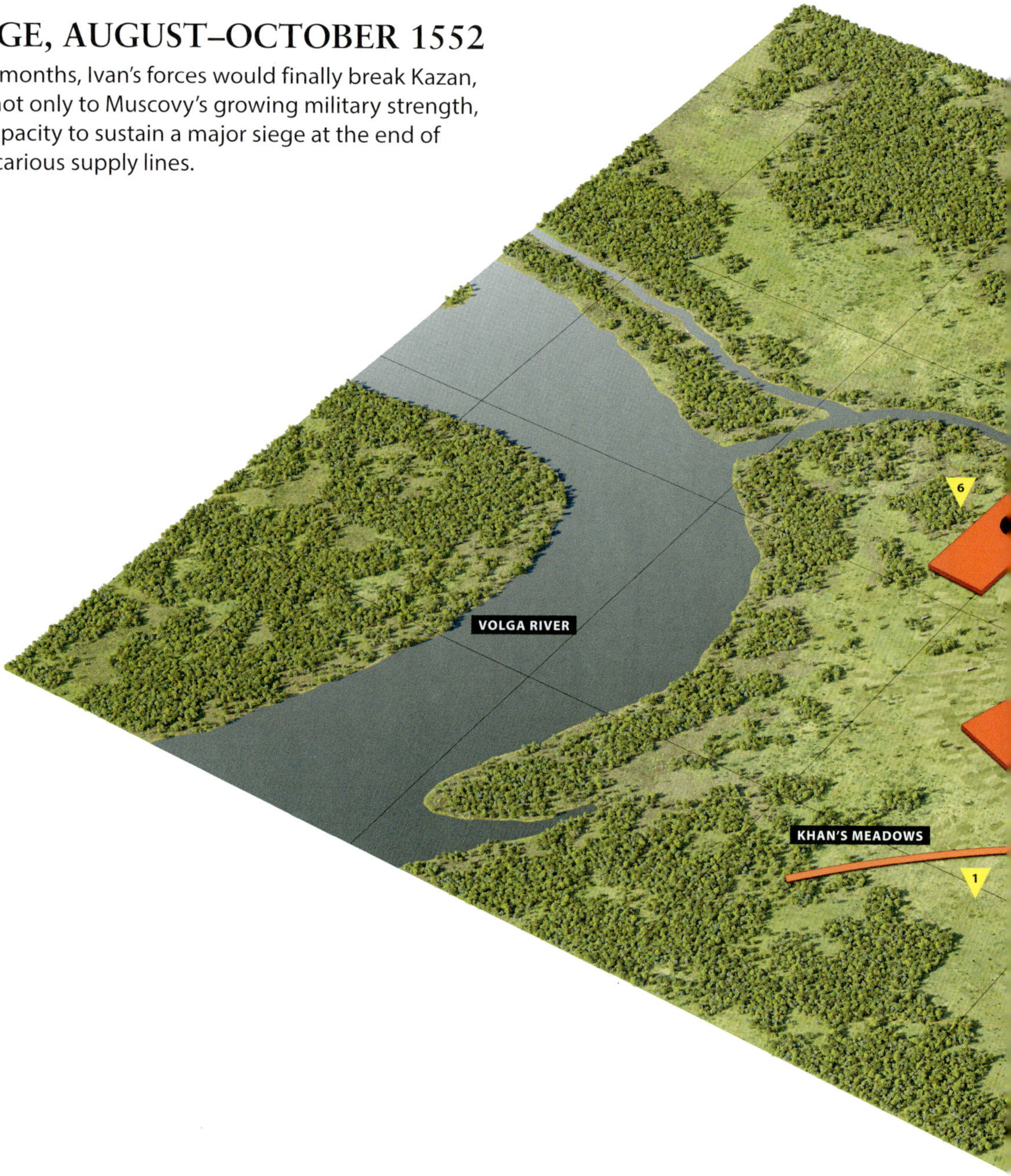

VOLGA RIVER

KHAN'S MEADOWS

▼ EVENTS

The Russians arrive

1. The Muscovite army arrives; Ivan sets up camp on Archa Field (23 August)
2. Major sortie against the Yertaul
3. Yapanchi's raids
4. Force sent to quell Yapanchi's forces
5. Cheremis harrassment

The siege

6. Muscovite forces take up their positions around Kazan
7. Siege lines established
8. Mine destroys Water Gate (4 September)
9. Sortie attempting to destroy Vyrodkov's siege tower; Russians take Archa Gate (26 September)
10. Mine under walls (30 September)

The assault

11. Mines breach the walls; Muscovite forces break into Kazan (2 October)
12. Ivan forced to enter city
13. Final assault on the Khan's Palace

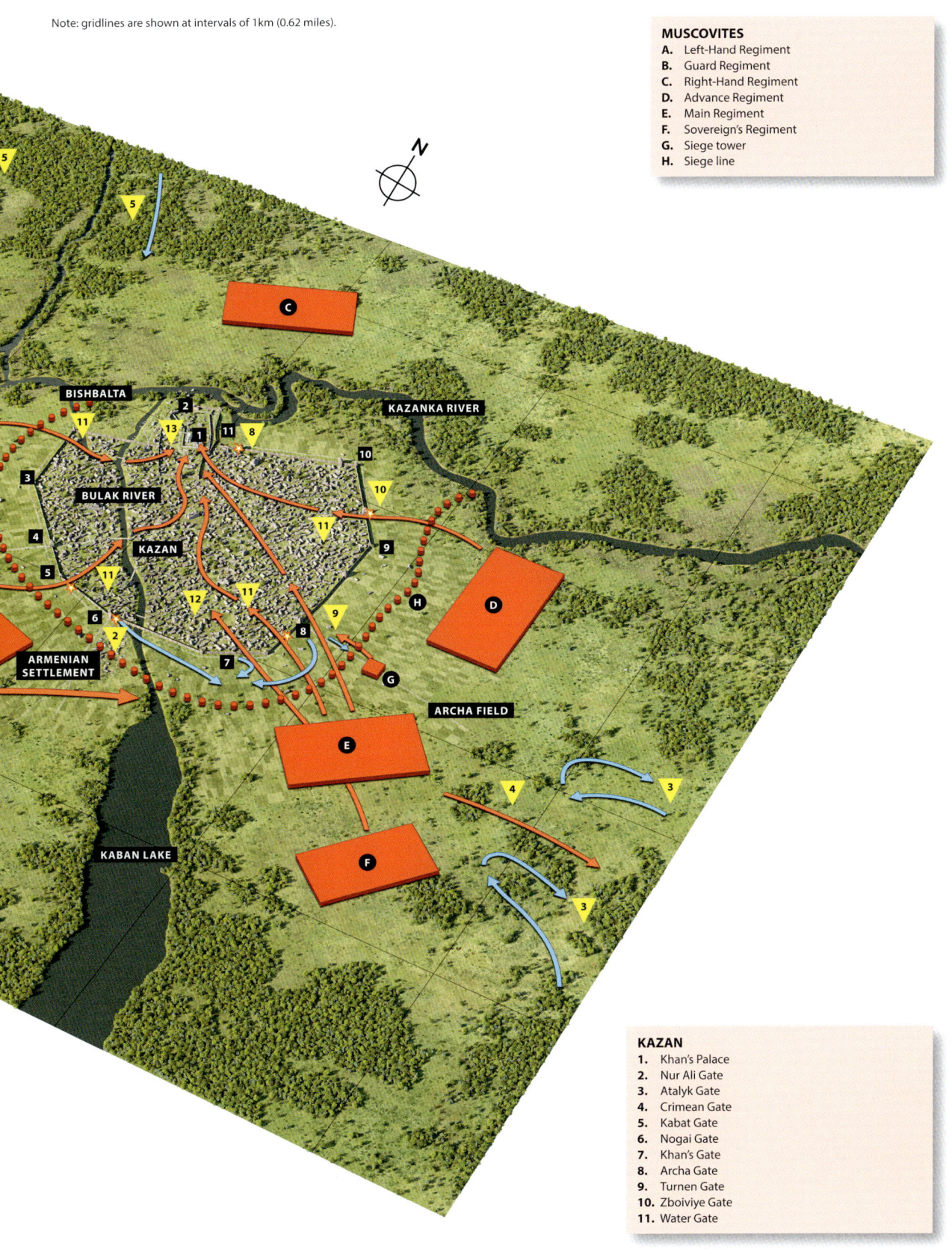

This was a time of transition, and *Streltsy* fought alongside soldiers such as this, who were scarcely different in their equipment or the tactics used from their medieval ancestors. Note the distinctive spiked helmet and round breastplate. (From The New York Public Library 1590594)

the Archa and Khan's Gates, right in front of the Main Regiment, was breached. Given that the storming of the city did not seem especially suited to light cavalry, the Qasimov Tatar contingent was deployed to protect the rear of the Russian camp on Archa Field, in case there was still some lurking reserve. Otherwise, Ivan's forces were to be committed en masse. The assault began, with *poshoshnye lyudi* hurling their simple bridges – little more than platforms of planks – over the defensive ditch. The Tatars held their fire until the last minute, before blasting the attackers with their surviving cannon, and from every bow and arquebus they could muster. Many Russians dropped, but they came on, sensing that the end of the siege was finally in sight. As they approached the walls, the Tatars hailed stones upon them, and poured boiling pitch from the surviving towers, although they were quickly silenced by Russian guns. The Muscovite forces nonetheless forced their way through the defence, with *murza* Chapkyn Otuchev the first of Kazan's leaders to fall to the swords of the Left-Hand Regiment, as it broke through at the Kabat Gate.

The *Kazan Chronicle*, whose unnamed author claimed to have consulted eyewitnesses who were there, paints a picture of chaos and carnage:

> And the Kazanians heard the sounds of trumpets from all the Russian regiments. And the Russians came from all sides, with all their strength, horsemen and footmen, and broke down all the gates of the fort, and they cut down the Kazanians – some sleeping, others running, as if mad, throwing themselves into the fire, forgetting about their horses and not remembering their weapons.

It certainly does seem that, once they had fought their way into the city, the Russians did not face any organized resistance, although much passionate disorganized resistance. As the attackers cut down the milling mob of remaining Kazan militia, the remaining Tatar soldiers fell back towards the Khan's Palace and its largely intact defences. Inside the maze of narrow and crooked streets, the Muscovites began to falter. In those close quarters, a Kazan local with a knife or a cleaver was arguably as well placed as a Russian soldier with a spear. More to the point, many of the attackers began looting, and it was harder for commanders to assert their authority once half their men were inside shops or round corners. Indeed, in his subsequent – and highly critical – *History of the Great Prince of Moscow*, Prince Andrei Kurbsky claimed that the opportunity for plunder attracted into the city *pososhnye lyudi*, camp followers and even shirkers who were playing dead or claiming to be more seriously wounded than they really were:

> … and those who were feigning, the so-called wounded, jumped up, and the fallen were raised from the dead. And from all quarters everyone, even those from the camps, the cooks, and the grooms, and others who had come with the army, they all rushed into the city, not to fight, but in the search of great gain…

Meanwhile, amidst this turmoil, soldiers took wrong turnings or simply took the opportunity to catch their breath after the hard fighting at the wall. One way or another, the attackers lost their momentum and the Tatars rallied. In a series of skirmishes that allowed them to gather scattered bands of surviving soldiers together, under Khan Ediger-Magmet himself, they began to push the Russians back from the palace. Facing this unexpected counterattack while they were dispersed and in disarray, the Muscovites, unaware of how far they still outnumbered the defenders, wavered. Kurbsky wrote that:

> Those aforementioned greedy ones, when they saw that ours were yielding little by little in their fight with the infidels, out of necessity, immediately took flight such that many could not even squeeze through the gates; but the majority rushed over the wall and others threw down even their plunder…

Where had Ivan been all this time? He had been attending a private religious service at the time, praying for victory. To his supporters, he was making manifest the tsar's role as the Russians' intermediary with God. To his critics – who would go on to include Andrei Kurbsky – it was a mark of cowardice or a dereliction of duty. He later wrote that Ivan had had to be compelled, that 'taking his horse by the bridle, they placed the tsar himself, whether he liked it or not, near the banner'. It may have been all of the above: Ivan's piety was undeniable, but he certainly did not appear eager to throw himself into the thick of battle, although others of his contemporaries believed he was not lacking in personal courage. Fortunately for the Russians, as their casualties mounted and their men teetered on the edge of panic,

The evolution of Russian helmets in this time: right to left, a classic conical helmet (worn with a quilted *tegilyai*), the compound helmet showing Lithuanian influence that was fashionable for a while in northern cities, and the simpler round helmet coming to be adopted by the latter half of the 16th century. (Public domain via Wikimedia Commons)

The representation of the siege in the *Illuminated Compiled Chronicle* tellingly portrays both sides' soldiers looking much the same. Even in this, the closest thing one could imagine to an 'official' representation, Ivan, in the background and distinguishable by his crown, remains in the safety of his camp at this stage. (Fine Art Images/Heritage Images/Getty Images)

at this point the service ended. The young tsar, who was already in armour, mounted his horse and led the Sovereign's Regiment into Kazan through the rubble of the Khan's Gate under Donskoi's banner.

The sight of the tsar – and the influx of fresh troops – went some way towards restoring the Russians' morale. Meanwhile, the voivodes and *sotniki* were desperately trying to reform their hundreds and reassert control, summarily cutting down a number of looters to make the point. The tide of battle turned yet again, and the khan reluctantly ordered a general withdrawal. Some 3,000 Tatar soldiers, as well as many desperate civilians, made it into the fortified complex that was the Khan's Palace before its metal-bound oaken doors were slammed and barred.

ENDGAME

The Khan's Palace was nowhere near as well-protected as the outer walls, though. Its wooden ramparts were soon being put to the torch or even being battered by a light cannon, a *tyufyak*, that had been manhandled through Kazan's streets. Forces from the Left-Hand and Guard Regiments, which had entered the city from the west and had to fight their way across the Bulak River, began to assault the small tower at the south-western corner of the palace's outer wall, while the Main Regiment stormed the main gatehouse to the south. Soldiers from the Right-Hand Regiment stationed on the banks of the Kazanka River to the north, who until now had played only a limited role in the attack, blasted the remnants of the Nur Ali Gate and may have actually been the first to break into the actual palace precincts. Certainly that was Pyotr Shchenyatev's subsequent proud boast.

What followed was a confused and bloody brawl, in which the defenders had no real hope of victory but hoped at least to fall with their swords bloody. The fighting cohered around three buildings within the palace walls: the khan's actual palace, the Kul Sharif Mosque and the ruins of the Nur Ali Gate. *Murza* Zaynash, the commander of the Nogai contingent, had his horse shot from under him at the Nur Ali Gate as he tried to flee with the last of his men, and was taken prisoner. There appears no reliable account of his life subsequently, so it is likely he was later executed, as not simply an enemy of Muscovy but, so the diplomatic fiction went, a traitor to his own khan.

At the palace, the Russians were soon battering at its doors with beams of wood left when the precinct walls were broken by cannon.

DEFEAT OF THE KHAN OF KAZAN.

Later, Western representations of the battle for Kazan tended to place them within an anachronistic chivalric tradition, such as this engraving which portrayed it as an open-field clash between medieval European-style knights and defenders on camel-back! (mikroman6 via Getty Images)

Khan Ediger-Magmet, with a picked guard of his most faithful Nogais, eventually retreated to a tower (some chronicles say they managed to make it to a hill outside the city). Either the khan surrendered to soldiers from the Sovereign's Regiment, on receiving promises of honourable captivity for him, his brothers and his surviving handful of men, or else he was handed over by his erstwhile protectors, trading him for their lives. Either way, he was quickly bound and manhandled out of the city.

The final fight was around the Kul Sharif Mosque, where a mix of Tatar soldiers and Kazan citizens continued their defiance, urged on by Kul Sharif himself. Their backbone was stiffened by the presence of several hundred of his own supporters, most of whom were determined to die rather than submit to the infidel. The elegantly paved square around the building was soon slick with blood, and Kul Sharif himself would not survive the battle. Again, accounts vary as to whether he cast himself from the roof of the mosque rather than be taken prisoner, or was killed atop it and it was his lifeless corpse which fell. Either way, with his death, the last remnants of organized resistance quickly dissipated. Russian soldiers roared into the mosque, defacing and looting in a mix of religious fervour and greedy relief. Another handful of defenders tried to cut their way to

THE FINAL DEFENCE, 2 OCTOBER 1552 (PP. 72–73)

A mixed force of Muscovite *Streltsy*, levy infantry and *dyeti boyarskiye* **(1)** have fought their way into the compound of the khan's residence, itself a fortified complex within the Khan's Palace. Encouraged by Prince Alexander Gorbaty-Shuisky **(2)**, they prepare to charge an equally motley collection of defenders and while Khan Ediger-Magmet is currently in the melee **(3)**, his personal guards are about to usher him to what will be only temporary safety in his tower **(4)**. *Oghlan* Aq Muhammad, who clearly realizes that all is lost, prepares to fight his way out **(5)**, a smart decision that will ensure he is one of the few commanders of the Kazan forces who will survive. The courtyard is already strewn with bodies, and a heated Russian cannonball has set on fire one of the buildings on the square, the residence of one of the khan's trusted relatives.

A modern representation by Firinat Khalikov (Xalikov) shows Kul Sharif, Koran held above his head, encouraging his students and followers as they defend their mosque in the final struggle for Kazan. (Firinat Khalikov, public domain, via Wikimedia Commons)

freedom over the Kazanka River, but were caught between their pursuers and the remaining elements of the Right-Hand Regiment under Andrei Kurbsky. Aq Muhammad, who had led the daring but doomed attempt to burn Vyrodkov's siege tower, did manage to escape to the Nogai Khanate, from whence he would travel to Crimea, where he was engaged by Khan Devlet Giray. Those Kazan defenders who could began to surrender, but it seems likely that they were more likely to be killed in the frenzy of the moment than allowed to live.

Kazan had fallen in a day's bloody fighting. The attackers lost 15,000 dead according to the *Kazan Chronicle*, but given that it claimed they numbered 150,000 in the first place, this ironically provides some indirect support for the generally accepted toll of 4,000–7,000 dead. Some reports put the Tatar losses at 5,000 dead, but the real butcher's bill was probably more like 20,000 dead, especially once one also includes the civilians who either took up arms or were simply caught in the crossfire. Thousands of Kazan's defenders were taken prisoner and deported to Russian lands where they were forced to convert and impressed into the Muscovite military.

Ivan did not tarry. He officiated over a formal service of thanksgiving, appointed Alexander Gorbaty-Shuisky as governor and Vasily Serebryany-Obolensky as his deputy, and on 11 October left for Moscow, as most of the army likewise returned either 'by the field' – by land – or else by barge back along the Volga, leaving just 3,000–4,000 troops behind, largely *Streltsy*. Many of Ivan's commanders urged leaving a larger garrison, but the tsar believed that for the moment the Tatars were too stunned by their defeat to resist. He was right up to a point, although soon enough resistance did begin to emerge.

This representation of Ivan the Terrible returning to Moscow after his conquest of Kazan owes more to his later appearance as he was just 22 at the time, but it does effectively portray the fashions and architecture of the time. (Universal History Archive/Universal Images Group via Getty Images)

Khan Ediger-Magmet was brought back to Moscow as hostage and prisoner, and the traditional regalia of the khans was appropriated by the tsar. As Ivan was returning to Moscow, he received the welcome news of the birth of his first son, Dmitry (although the young heir would accidentally drown just eight and a half months later) and he was greeted in the capital by cheering crowds. He held a feast for his commanders and showered them with gifts (some of his plunder from Kazan), from furs to horses, and was hailed as the champion of Christendom. Kazan was indeed now a Muscovite possession – but holding it would prove a continuing challenge.

AFTERMATH

> Ediger comes looking like a slave:
> His head bowed on his chest,
> Covered in ash, trembling, frank;
> His groaning chest is washed by a stream of tears:
> Having found his path from the kingdom blocked by warriors,
> Desperate, pale, poor, and in tattered rags,
> He fell down, wept, and prostrated himself before Ivan;
> Beating his forehead in the dust, before the feet of the Monarch,
> He says: Look no more for the Tsar of Kazan!
> He is no more! He is no more! … You are the King of this realm
> – *Rossiyada*

Once the bodies had been collected from the streets of Kazan and a rough and ready order established, Ivan promised its surviving inhabitants – those not killed or forcibly resettled – competent and even-handed government, commending Gorbaty-Shuisky and Vasily Serebryany-Obolensky to them as

This particular idealized rendition of the fall of Kazan by Pyotr Shamshin does again at least show Ivan as a 22-year-old, although Ediger-Magmet, the figure at the centre in white robes about to submit, is distinctly too clean and collected considering what he has just been through. (Fine Art Images/Heritage Images/Getty Images)

his 'good, fair representatives', along with the administrator Ivan Bezsonov. Although the Kul Sharif Mosque was demolished as a potential symbol of resistance and plans for a new Christian cathedral quickly advanced, initially there were serious attempts to reconcile the conquered Tatars with their new masters. This would not last long, though, and a campaign of insurrection would usher in an era of repression and forced Russification that would essentially set the tone of relations through to the reign of Catherine the Great in the late 18th century.

GUERRILLA WAR, 1552–56

In hindsight, it was clear that those older and wiser heads who had counselled Ivan to spend more time in his new territories and, above all, leave behind a much more substantial force, were right. Soon after the fall of Kazan, many of the leaders of Tatar tribes and other peoples who had been subject to the khan began to become restive. Some resented the arrival of Christians, others saw this as an opportunity for plunder. Gorbaty-Shuisky had been left with enough troops to garrison the city, but not also to carry out punitive raids and deterrent patrols in force in Kazan's hinterland, especially as most of his troops were slow-moving infantry rather than cavalry. Although he was aware of the growing challenge, there was little he could do about it beyond fulminate and send increasingly more urgent dispatches to distant Moscow. Ivan was impatient and unsympathetic, not least as he was already turning his mind to a follow-on campaign against the Astrakhan Khanate.

Tentative raids led to more serious attacks, and Muscovite officials travelling far from Kazan had to be assigned larger and larger detachments of guards. Kurbsky presents what emerged as an open and full-blown rebellion:

The irony is that those who submitted to the tsars – such as Kuchum Khan of the Siberian Khanate, here being paraded into Moscow – were often treated well and saw their peoples retain a degree of cultural autonomy. (© Fine Art Images/Heritage/TopFoto)

> The remaining princes of Kazan rose up against the tsar and, together with other pagan peoples, attacked not only Kazan itself, but also, through the great forests, raided the lands around Murom and even Nizhny Novgorod itself, and took captives. And so it was continuously after the capture of the Kazan kingdom, for about six years, during which all the newly established cities in that land, and some in Russia, were besieged by them.

In fairness, though, he had an axe to grind given that he had been amongst those advocating for a larger garrison. Instead of this full-scale revolt, there were raids deeper into Muscovite territory, and what ensued was closer to a guerrilla war, where princes protested loyalty to the tsar while ever looking for a chance to ambush some merchants or tax collectors or dry gulch a courier. The more they could act with impunity, though, the more confident they became, until most of the territories along the southern left bank of the Kazanka River were in revolt. By 1554, this had spread such that most of Kazan's hinterland was, if not controlled by the rebels – to whose numbers had flocked other Tatars, Meadow Cheremis and Udmurts – certainly not in Moscow's hands. The rebels established their own fortified strongholds at Mishätamaq, 40 miles south of Kazan at the confluence of the Myosha and Kama Rivers, and Chalem, on the right bank of the Volga.

Initial Russian responses were often hasty and inadequate. When voivode Boris Saltykov attacked Mishätamaq in 1553 with little more than a thousand men, his force was defeated and he was killed in the fight, his body left in the snows. The rebels would suffer from a lack of coordination, however. Even the most influential figure within the rebellion, Mameshbirde, was unable to unite them fully, and tried inviting the khan of the Nogai, Ismail, to become their leader. It was an offer he could refuse, but he hedged his bets by allowing – or encouraging – some of his men to join the uprising, albeit without open support, so as to retain deniability.

Moscow held Kazan, though, and by 1553, Ivan had agreed to send in more troops, including light cavalry better equipped to respond to the rebels' hit-and-run tactics. In February 1554, Prince Semyon Mikulinsky led a large punitive force out of Kazan and scoured the rebel-held areas to the east and north of the city. Thousands of prisoners were taken, and settlements suspected of feeding and harbouring the rebels were destroyed. Contingents were raised across Muscovy to send to Kazan, and a new fortress was built at Cheboksary, on the Volga river route to Kazan, to guard its supply lines. Rebel attempts to prevent its construction were bloodily repulsed.

This low-level rebellion would finally be suppressed in 1556: Mishätamaq and Chalem were levelled, Mameshbirde captured during an ill-planned campaign in the territories of the Mountain Cheremis (and later executed in Moscow) and remaining larger rebel forces dispersed or destroyed. A key factor was the arrival in 1555 of a new duumvirate in Kazan: the competent and energetic Prince Pyotr Shuisky and, instead of another prince, Archbishop Gury, who had been appointed the head of the new cathedral and diocese. Shuisky completed the military portion of the campaign to crush the rebellion, while the Gury oversaw an equally ruthless campaign of Russification, cracking down on the remaining Muslim clergy,

Although revered as a saint in the Orthodox Church, the evidence suggests that Archbishop Gury (Gurias), in his 11 years presiding over the Kazan diocese, implemented a sometimes unyielding campaign of Russification and enforced conversion. (Fine Art Images/Heritage Images/TopFoto)

encouraging grandees to send their children into Muscovy to be educated in the ways of the conquerors and generally trying to assimilate those within the Tatar elite willing to play ball, and repressing the others. Many of the latter group would have their lands sequestered and from 1557 these were distributed to a new collection of *pomeshchik* service gentry, who would also be Moscow's local eyes, ears and, if necessary, strong right arm.

The consequences of the war were severe for the former khanate. The economy experienced a steep decline, not least because of depopulation. Promises made to the Tatars about their continued equal status in Kazan before the revolt were revoked, and many were expelled from the city. A new ruling elite of Russified Tatars and incoming Muscovite officials took power. Nonetheless, the city's prime location along the Volga trade routes ensured that it would soon recover, and it was also ironically the beneficiary of further Russian campaigns, as a source of food and recruits.

THE CONQUEST OF ASTRAKHAN

Kazan was only the start of Ivan's ambitions to the south. Ideally, he wanted to bring all the khanates under his control, to end the slave raids and, even more importantly, prevent their becoming staging posts for Ottoman expansion towards Muscovy's underbelly. Ivan's plans to take Crimea would never come to fruition – that would end up taking another couple of centuries – but he quickly began seeking a *casus belli* for a first move against the Astrakhan Khanate. His correspondence with the newly elevated Khan Ismail of the Nogai, whom he consulted about how best to take Astrakhan, make it clear that he explicitly saw this as the first step to Crimea. Ismail, it has to be said, also had his own agenda for encouraging such a war, as he hoped to place his relative, Darwish Ghali, on Astrakhan's throne.

The aggressive Yamghurchi, khan of Astrakhan, who had usurped power from Aq Kübek in 1550 with Nogai assistance, could not help himself from giving Ivan such a pretext. Originally, he offered his fealty to Moscow, and as a result Ivan sent as an ambassador Sevastian Avraamov. However, it seems that Yamghurchi had hoped to gain personally from the seizure of Kazan (even though he had provided no support) and no longer felt the need to

Beyond Kazan, later 16th century

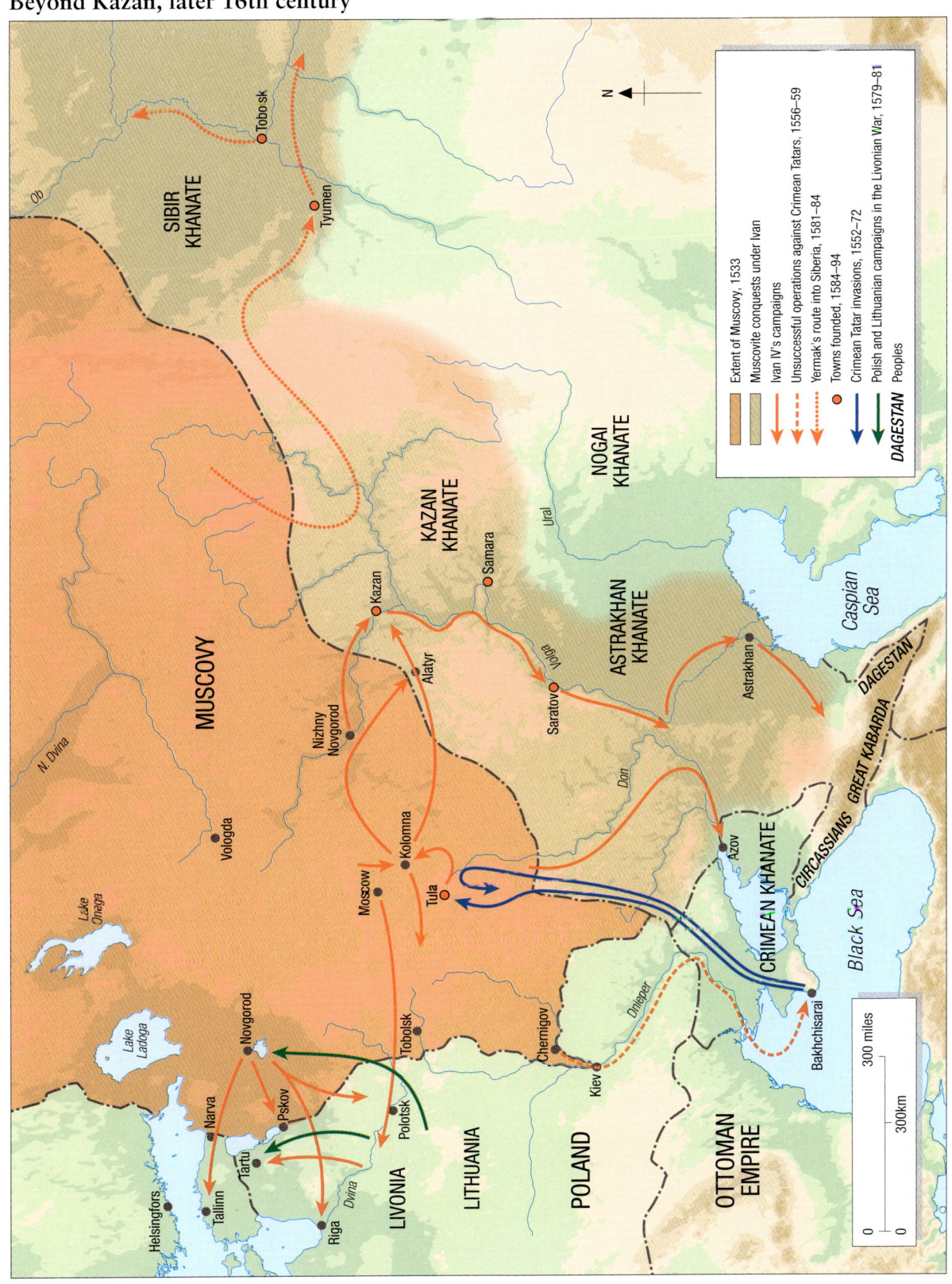

Astrakhan was also a slave market, and a secondary goal was to prevent the continued raids for *yasyr*, slaves, who would be led to Astrakhan lashed together in great coffles, in which the weak, old and infirm might well die in their chains. (Erhard Schön, public domain, via Wikimedia Commons)

make good on his promises of vassalage. When Avraamov arrived in 1554, according to the Dutch envoy and grain trader, he 'was treated very badly, even worse than the envoys of King David sent to Annon, the king of the Ammonites, and, on top of that, was driven out of Astrakhan with ridicule'. Nor was ridicule the worst: Avraamov's property was seized, and he was imprisoned on an island in the Caspian Sea. Ivan was at once relieved to have his excuse, but also genuinely angry. Avraamov was his representative, and this was a slight to the notoriously touchy young monarch's honour. Massa wrote that he swore 'to raze Astrakhan to the ground before winter comes, and to show no mercy to anyone anymore, and … to put everyone to the sword'.

That spring, an army of 30,000 Muscovite troops under Prince Yuri Pronsky-Shemyakin set out down the Volga towards Astrakhan. The Advance Regiment, under Alexander Vyazemsky and Danila Chulkov, encountered the vanguard of Yamghurchi's army on reconnaissance: near Cherny Island, the advance detachment encountered the Astrakhan vanguard under the command of Sakmak, who had himself been delegated to locating the Muscovite force. The Tatars were trapped against the fast-flowing Volga and all but wiped out. Sakmak was taken prisoner, and from him the Russians learned that Astrakhan itself was virtually abandoned, and Yamghurchi had taken up positions at one of the branches of the Volga delta (on the Tsarevaya channel) some five miles south of the city. His plan was to wait until the Russians surrounded the city and then attack them from behind.

Forewarned, Pronsky-Shemyakin sent the Advance Regiment, reinforced by the personal retinues of several powerful voivodes, to engage

Yamghurchi, while he secured the city. This proved no real challenge, sparsely defended as it was. As Russian troops encircled it, most of the remaining troops there fled, and Astrakhan was taken essentially without resistance, allowing Pronsky-Shemyakin to send Vyazemsky further reinforcements. They were hardly needed: Yamghurchi fled east to the Ottoman fortress of Azov, and without their khan the Astrakhan forces, which in any case numbered fewer than 10,000 men, were in little mood to put up a fight.

Massa, who was writing decades later, claimed that while:

> Astrakhan was very fortified by nature itself, populous and supplied with weapons, a few days later it was taken by storm, all men and women were exterminated by the sword, also children, and … so it was destroyed to the ground without any mercy…

A representation of the fall of Astrakhan from the *Illustrated Chronicle of Ivan the Terrible*. (Facial Chronicle [Illustrated Chronicle of Ivan the Terrible], public domain, via Wikimedia Commons)

This was something of an exaggeration. It is certainly true that much of the original city, that had been built on the higher right bank of the Volga, almost seven miles upstream from the current city (in a location now known as Shareny Bugor), had been destroyed, but the city did survive, not least because its defenders had put up so little a fight. Darwish Ghali, who had accompanied the army, was duly installed as the new khan, releasing thousands of Russian slaves and pledging his fealty to Ivan and promising to pay an annual tribute of 40,000 gold altyns and 3,000 fine sturgeons from the Volga. Pronsky-Shemyakin stayed in Astrakhan for a month before returning to Moscow in triumph, leaving behind a garrison under voivode Pyotr Turgenev.

At Azov, Yamghurchi began lobbying the Ottomans to reinstall him on the throne. In 1555, he led an army comprised of Crimean and Nogai Tatars and Turkish Janissaries back towards Astrakhan and tried to retake it. This came to little: Muscovite forces in the khanate were reinforced and loyalist Nogai also rallied to their side. After a

A panorama of Russian Astrakhan in the 18th century, across the Volga River. Note the traditional Tatar yurt on cart in the foreground, a slightly fanciful gesture even though they were still in use in the hinterland. (PHAS/Universal Images Group via Getty Images)

month of confused, sporadic skirmishes, Yamghurchi was forced to retreat: his supply lines were overstretched, his troops were getting mutinous and there seemed no prospect of an easy win. Instead, the Ottomans, working through their Crimean allies, tried corruption and diplomacy. In 1556, they persuaded Darwish Ghali to renounce Moscow and drive its representative, Leonty Mansurov, out of the city. The plan was apparently to reinforce the city with a Crimean army, but Ismail of the Nogai, his nose out of joint at this betrayal of his interests, too, tipped Ivan off soon enough that a Russian army under Ivan Cheremisinov, first commander of the Moscow *Streltsy*, supported by Cossack horsemen under Mikhail Kolupayev, could get there first. Hearing this news, Darwish Ghali fled Astrakhan, putting what was left of it to the torch. He and his troops tried to make a stand on the floodplains of the Volga delta, and while there were moments in the ensuing battle in which the Tatars gave a good account of themselves, they were outnumbered, outgunned and were unable to use the flexible and mobile tactics that were their forte, especially as the *Streltsy* fought behind a *gulyai-gorod*. By the end of the day, Darwish Ghali was following in Yamghurchi's footsteps and fleeing to Azov.

Ivan was resolved to be done with unreliable Tatar vassals and instead to bring Astrakhan into his direct rule. With the old city all but ruined, he decided on the construction of a wooden kremlin to be the basis of a new one. The decision was made in 1558 to build it on the site of what is now the centre of the city, and in 1559, while returning from Bukhara, the English merchant and diplomat Anthony Jenkinson found it already standing 'on an island, on a high bank with a castle inside the city, surrounded by an earthen rampart and wooden walls'. Even by then, though, a larger, stone kremlin was being built, which would be completed by 1589, giving Moscow a strongpoint along the trade routes to Asia and to guard against a flank attack from Crimea.

This 60-ruble stamp commemorating 450 years since the Battle of Molodi shows in the foreground Mikhail Vorotynsky in the classic armour and helmet of a Russian heavy cavalryman, and in the background Muscovite soldiers fighting from behind a *gulyai-gorod* and Ivan's personal banner. (Beltyukov V., public domain, via Wikimedia Commons)

GREAT POWER, GREAT RIVALS

Ivan's conquests of the Kazan and Astrakhan Khanates were triumphs, but dangerous ones. The entire Middle Volga region was annexed, and peoples who had either been subjects of the khanates or semi-independent, including the Cheremis and the Bashkirs, were now subjects of Moscow. The Nogai realized that their days of being able to play off rival powers were at an end. In 1563, the Siberian Khanate would peacefully become a tributary of Moscow.

However, this brought the Russians into more direct contact and competition with the Ottomans, another empire on the rise. This rivalry would endure for centuries. Indeed, it built on Moscow's claim to be the 'Third Rome' after Christian Constantinople had fallen to Islam and Sultan Mehmed II in 1453. In 1569, the Turks would send an army of 20,000 of their own troops (including 15,000 Janissaries) and 50,000 Crimean Tatars to lay siege to Astrakhan. Thus opened the first of many Russo-Turkish wars that would be fought over the coming centuries. Despite the scale of the Ottoman force – one Russian defender noted that as 'other regiments marched on the sides, in front and behind and from the sides, that the entire field was covered with so many that I could not see them from the highest vantage' – they were unable to take Astrakhan before a Russian relief army arrived. Nonetheless, in 1571, the Crimean

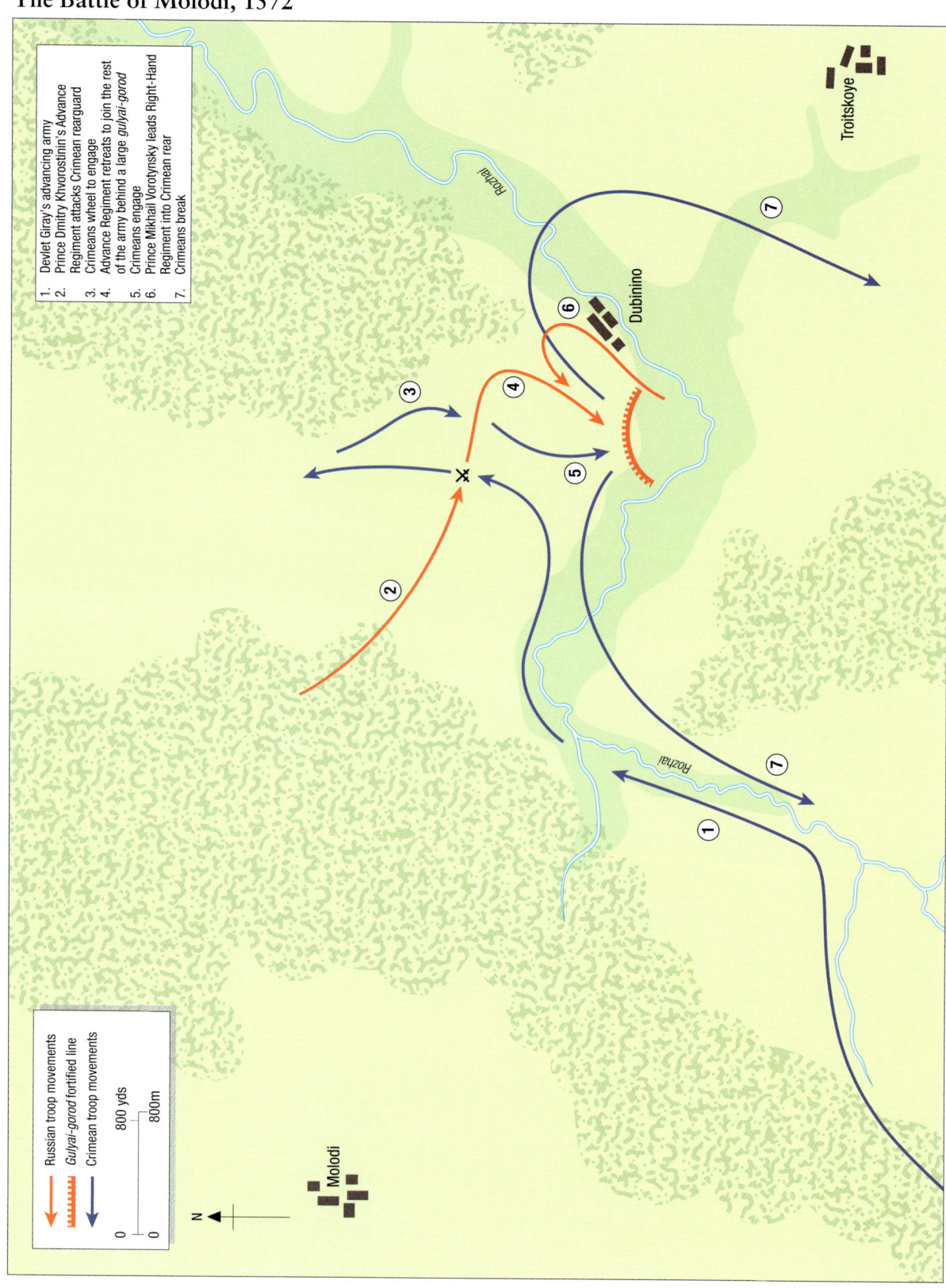

Tatars, once more with Ottoman assistance, were able to make it all the way to Moscow. Although again they lacked the guns and siegecraft to take it, they did put much of the wooden-built city to the torch. The year after, Khan Devlet Giray tried again with an even larger army – and was conclusively defeated in the Battle of Molodi, after which bloodletting the Crimeans would be unable to pose any serious threat to Muscovy for the next two decades.

The Russian Army Capturing Narva on 11 May 1558, by Alexander Blinkov, depicts the seizure of this Estonian city during the Livonian War. Note the red swallowtail banner at the centre, evoking the Banner of the Most Merciful Saviour flown at Kazan. (Fine Art Images/Heritage Images/Getty Images)

The Battle of Molodi, 1572

The Battle of Molodi, fought some 50 miles south of Moscow, would be crucial in stabilizing the Russian grip on the south at a time when it was already weakened by the Livonian War. As usual, figures for the size of the respective armies are often exaggerated: the *Novgorod Second Chronicle* claims that Devlet Giray's army numbered 120,000 and the *Moscow Chronicle* even put it as 150,000. Modern research suggests a still-substantial 60,000, two thirds of whom were Crimean troops, along with perhaps 7,000 Ottoman Janissaries and the rest being made up by Nogai, Circassians and other allied or mercenary detachments. Against them, Muscovy could muster almost 25,000 under Prince Mikhail Vorotynsky, for which we have unusually precise records for once: 8,255 in the Main Regiment, along with some 3,000–5,000 Cossacks under their ataman Mikhail Cherkashenin, 3,950 in the Right-Hand Regiment, 4,475 in the Advance Regiment and 4,650 in the Guard. In this engagement, only four regiments were able to be deployed. Despite being outnumbered, the Russians were able to engage with the invaders when they were still strung out in march order. Even as their van was some ten miles ahead, their rearguard was attacked by the Russian Advance Regiment under Prince Dmitry Khvorostinin. Unwilling to leave his rear vulnerable, Devlet Giray swung to meet Khvorostinin's forces, which undertook a planned retreat to where the Main Regiment was waiting under the protection of a large *gulyai-gorod*. Two days of successive assaults against the fortified Russians left them bled and exhausted, but Devlet Giray increasingly desperate. As he threw even dismounted cavalry into the melee, this permitted Vorotynsky to lead the Right-Hand Regiment out of their defensive lines unnoticed, through a ravine, and into a perfect position to attack the Crimeans from the rear. At the same time, Khvorostinin's troops made a desperate sortie from the *gulyai-gorod*, under a barrage of cannon fire that all but exhausted the Russians' reserves, but nonetheless helped disrupt the Crimeans. They broke and fled. Their casualties were terrible, including almost all the Janissaries, as well as most of the Crimean *murzas*, and even Devlet Giray's son, grandson and son-in-law.

The Crimean Khanate, increasingly nothing but an Ottoman subject, would survive thanks to this support until 1783. The real importance of Moscow's new rivalry with the Turks to the south-west, though, was that it coincided with its continuing struggles in the north-west over access to the Baltic Sea. In 1558, the Livonian War would see Moscow fighting first the Livonian Confederation but then also an alliance which would include Sweden, Lithuania, Denmark and Poland. Early successes gave way to a series of defeats and Moscow had eventually to concede defeat. Nonetheless, what this did mean was that at the very time it was facing the increasingly powerful and assertive Ottomans, they were also engaged in a long-term, off-and-on struggle with some of the more advanced nations of northern Europe. Ivan had wanted to assert Muscovy's status as a great power, and he had achieved that – but at the cost of embroiling it in new and ever-more dangerous regional rivalries.

Bakhchisarai, once the capital of the Crimean Khanate but seized by the Russians in 1783, is now a small and sleepy town, best known for the Hansaray, the Khan's Palace, and the Büyük Han Cami, the Big Khan Mosque. (Sean Gallup/Getty Images)

THE BATTLEFIELD TODAY

> The renewed city raised its head;
> The waves cleansed the blood on the riverbanks;
> The forests and mountains seemed full of joy.
> – *Rossiyada*

The conquest of Kazan really marks the point at which an essentially Russian Muscovite state began to become a multi-ethnic, multi-confessional empire. Tatar aristocrats, some notionally converted to Christianity, but some not, would be incorporated into the elite. (And to symbolize his victory over a Muslim khanate, Ivan decreed that henceforth the crescent should be placed underneath the Christian cross atop the domes of Orthodox churches.) Ediger-Magmet would in due course be baptized as Semyon in a grand public event that saw him and his household be elevated into the ranks of the boyars. Utamish Giray, son of Safa Giray, was baptized as Alexander and brought into Ivan's own household, as something between a hostage and a guest. His mother, Söyembikä, was more defiant and was eventually married off – not necessarily willingly – to Shigalei, the khan of the Kasim Tatars. The pragmatic Muscovite system, itself influenced by both Mongol and Russian political traditions, proved willing and able to incorporate all who might be useful into its ruling class.

The city itself is now the capital of the Republic of Tatarstan, a constituent element of the Russian Federation, and Kazan is known as the 'Third Capital of Russia' after Moscow and St Petersburg. It was captured by Cossack

The Kazan Kremlin now, showing the minarets of the rebuilt Kul Sharif Mosque, the onion domes of the Cathedral of the Annunciation and the leaning Söyembikä Tower. (© Mark Galeotti)

Much of Kazan's Tatar heritage has been subsumed within a greater Russian and Soviet culture, but events such as the celebration of the victory over Nazi Germany – here showing the 75th anniversary in 2020 – cross the ethnic and cultural divides. (Maksim Bogodvid – Host Photo Agency via Getty Images)

rebels during the Pugachyov Rebellion (1773–75), and was largely destroyed as a result, but was soon rebuilt and developed as one of the country's great cities, with a distinctive mix of Russia and Tatar influences. It was far enough from the frontlines to be largely unscathed during World War II and, indeed, became an industrial hub, as factories were evacuated from further west. Tatars make up a bare majority of the population of the city, with the indigenous Russian population coming a close second, but interethnic relations these days are relatively harmonious.

Little is left of 16th-century Kazan, not least as so much of it was made of wood and burnt down during the siege itself. At the city's heart, where the Khan's Palace once stood, Ivan decreed the construction of a fortress, a kremlin, as both a mark of his victory and a defensive bastion for the new garrison and administration. In 1556, 200 masons from the city of Pskov arrived and began building it. By 1568 it was complete, a large enclosed area bounded by a stone wall and 13 towers, built in the Pskov architectural vernacular. Within this wall were numerous buildings, including the new Annunciation Cathedral, the oldest Orthodox church in the Middle Volga region. After the fall of the USSR in 1991, it was joined by the new Kul Sharif Mosque, modelled after its counterpart destroyed during the siege. The Söyembikä Tower, a seven-tiered structure that leans noticeably to the north-east, may be named after one of the last queens of independent Kazan, but is actually a later construction, which nonetheless did build on the foundations of the gatehouse of the inner precinct of the Tatar city. The winding, swampy Bulak is now just a short length of straight, still channel in downtown Kazan.

The irony is that one of the most distinctive Russian Orthodox churches, St Basil's on Red Square, owes much in style and gaudy colour to the Kul Sharif Mosque, which was destroyed on Ivan's orders, even as he commissioned this monument to the victory of Christendom over Islam. (© Mark Galeotti)

The city has a wealth of galleries and museums, the latter devoted to everything from tea to moonshine, but for insights into Tatar life and warfare in the 16th century, the National Museum of the Republic of Tatarstan and the Tatarskaya Sloboda Museum are the visitor's best bet, even if the information presented is not always translated into English. Nonetheless, commemorating the siege remains a complex political topic in Tatarstan. From the early 1990s, 15 October – the date of the city's fall in 1552 in the current Gregorian calendar – was informally known as the Day of Remembrance and Sorrow of the Tatar People. Some even portrayed the defenders as *shahids*, martyrs, who died in the name of their faith, and comparing Ivan IV with Hitler, and the sacking of Kazan to the Nazis' planned destruction of Moscow and Leningrad. During the heyday of secessionism, in the early 1990s, placards with slogans such as 'I remember 1552' and '1555 – the Holocaust of the Tatar people!' would often be brandished during

Kazan would play its role in World War II as a vital industrial hub, even repairing captured Axis tanks for use by the Red Army, and as the HQ of the 18th Rifle Division, which was functionally destroyed when encircled by advancing German forces in August 1941. (Engelberthumperdink, CC BY-SA 4.0 https://creativecommons.org/licenses/by-sa/4.0, via Wikimedia Commons)

protests. Nonetheless, these last notions were soon considered too heretical and were largely pushed out of public discourse and, as Vladimir Putin's state became more centralized and authoritarian, especially after the 2022 invasion of Ukraine, scope for such displays of local identity, particularly in connection with Muscovite imperialism, quickly shrank. In 2024, the Day of Remembrance was officially scrubbed from the calendar, and independence marches banned and suppressed.

One of the most distinctive (and gaudy) remembrances of the war, though, is in Moscow: the Cathedral of the Intercession of the Most Holy Theotokos on the Moat, better known as St Basil's Cathedral, sitting at one end of Red Square. In 1555, Ivan ordered the construction of this extraordinary church, with its nine multi-coloured onion domes, to celebrate his triumphs over Kazan and Astrakhan, drawing on the example of Kazan's Kul Sharif Mosque.

FURTHER READING

Abduzhemilev, Refat, 'Remmal Khodzha, Khronika "Tarikh-I Sakhib Gerai khan" ("Istoriya o khane Sakhib Gerae")', ('Remmal Khodzha, The Chronicle "Tarikh-i Sahib Giray Khan" ["The Story of Khan Sahib Giray"]'), Part 3, *Krimskoe Istoricheskoe Obozrenie*, 1/2019 (2019)

Collins, Leslie, 'The Military Organization and Tactics of the Crimean Tatars During the Sixteenth and Seventeenth Centuries', in Vernon Parry and Malcolm Yapp (eds), *War, Technology and Society in the Middle East*, Oxford University Press (1975)

Crummey, Robert, *The Formation of Muscovy 1304–1613*, Longman (1987)

Davies, Brian, *Warfare, State and Society on the Black Sea Steppe, 1500–1700*, Routledge (2007)

Erusalimskii, K., *Kazanskii Pokhod Ivana Groznogo 1552 g* ('The Kazan Campaign of Ivan the Terrible 1552'), Institute of History named after Shigabutdin Mardzhani (2023)

Esper, Thomas, 'Military Self-Sufficiency and Weapons Technology in Muscovite Russia', *Slavic Review*, 28.2 (1969)

Filjushkin, Alexander, *Ivan the Terrible: A Military History*, Frontline (1988)

Galeotti, Mark, *Forged in War: A Military History of Russia from its Beginnings to Today*, Osprey (2024)

Gliwa, Andrzej, 'The Tatar Military Art of War in the Early Modern Period: an example of asymmetric warfare', *Acta Poloniae Historica*, 114 (2016)

Huttenbach, Henry, 'Muscovy's conquest of Muslim Kazan and Astrakhan, 1552–1556', in Michael Rywkin (ed.), *Russian Colonial Expansion to 1917*, Mansell (1988)

Khodarkovsky, Michael, 'Taming The "Wild Steppe": Muscovy's Southern Frontier, 1480–1600', *Russian History*, 26.3 (1999)

Khovanskaya, Olga, 'Pokhody Ivana Groznogo na Kazan' v 1549–1552 gg', ('Ivan the Terrible's campaigns against Kazan in 1549–1552) in Olga Khovanskaya (ed), *Osada i Vzyatie Kazani v 1552 godu* ('The Siege and Capture of Kazan in 1552'), MOiN RT (2010)

Medved, A. N., 'I snova o Svyazhskoi kreposti, 1551 g' ('And again about the Svyazhsk fortress, 1551'), *Arkheologiya Evrazskikh Stepei*, 5.2023 (2023)

Morrison, Alexander, *The Russian Conquest of Central Asia: A Study in Imperial Expansion, 1814–1914*, Cambridge University Press (2020)

Nicolle, David and Viacheslav Shpakovsky, *Armies of Ivan the Terrible: Russian Troops 1505–1700*, Osprey (2006)

Nossov, Konstantin, *Russian Fortresses 1480–1682*, Osprey (2006)

Paul, Michael, 'The Military Revolution in Russia, 1550–1682', *Journal of Military History*, 68.1 (2004)

Pavlov, Andrei and Maureen Perrie, *Ivan the Terrible*, Pearson (2003)

Pelenskyj, Jaroslav, *Russia and Kazan: Conquest and Imperial Ideology (1438–1560s)*, De Gruyter (2017)

Penskoi, Vitaly, *Ivan Grozny i Devlet-Girey* ('Ivan the Terrible and Devlet Giray'), Veche (2012)

Rayfield, Donald, *'A Seditious and Sinister Tribe': The Crimean Tatars and Their Khanate*, Reaktion (2024)

Romaniello, Matthew, *The Elusive Empire: Kazan and the Creation of Russia, 1552–1671*, University of Wisconsin Press (2012)

Ševčenko, Ihor, 'Muscovy's Conquest of Kazan: Two Views Reconciled', *Slavic Review*, 26.4 (1967)

Shpakovsky, Viacheslav and David Nicolle, *Armies of the Volga Bulgars & Khanate of Kazan: 9th–16th centuries*, Osprey (2013)

Smith, Dianne, 'Muscovite Logistics, 1462–1598', *Slavonic and East European Review*, 71.1 (1993)

Volkov, Vladimir and Rostislav Vvedensky, *Russko-kazanskaya voina 1547–1552 gg* ('The Russo-Kazan War, 1547–1552'), MPGU (2015)

Volkova, Tatyana, 'Chudo i ego vospriyatie geroyami «Kazanskoi istorii» – pravoslavnymi i musul'manami' ('A Miracle and Its Perception by the Heroes of "Kazan Chronicle" – Orthodox and Muslims'), *Problemy Istoricheskoi Poetiki*, 20.2 (2022)

Von Essen, Michael Fredholm, *Muscovy's Soldiers: The Emergence of the Russian Army 1462–1689*, Helion (2018)

Williams, Brian Glyn, *The Sultan's Raiders: The Military Role of the Crimean Tatars in the Ottoman Empire*, Jamestown Foundation (2013)

INDEX

Figures in **bold** refer to illustrations.

Adashev, Alexei 22–23
Alatyr **12**, 48–49, **81**
Aq Muhammad 63–64, **74**, 75
Archa (Arsk) 25–26, 51, 54–56
Archa Field 7, **43**, **44**, 54, **66–67**, 68
    Battle of Archa Field 54, 55
Archa Gate **43**, 44, 60, 63–65, **66–67**, 68
archers 33, 42, 45, 55, **57**, 63–64
armour 11, 26, **28**, **30**, **31**, 32, 34, **38**, **40**, 41–42, 50, **51**, 54, **61**, 70, 85
arquebuses 17, **28**, 31, 33–34, 56–57, 60, **61**, **62**, 68
arquebusiers 19, 64
artillery 17, 28–29, 31, **35**, 40, 54–55, **57**, **62**, 63
artillerymen **20**, 35–36, 62
Astrakhan 7, **9**, 19, 21, 24, 80, **81**, **82**, 83, **84**, 85, 92
Astrakhan Khanate **9**, 11, 21, 24–25, **47**, 78, 80, **81**, 85
Atalyk Gate **43**, 44, 65, **67**
Avraamov, Sevastian 80, 82
Azov **9**, **81**, 83–84

Basmanov, Alexei 30, **64**, 65
Battle of Molodi 21, **85**, **86**, 87
begs 6, 38
Bishbalta **8**, **43**, 67
bows **10**, **18**, **28**, 30, **32**, 33, 42, 50, 54, **57**, 68
boyars 5–6, 12–13, 22–23, **28**, 30–32, 89
Bukhara 6, 84
Bulgars 5, **6**, 38, **39**, 45
'Butler' 36, 63

cannon **13**, 17, 20, 31, **35**, **44**, **57**, 60, **61**, **62**, 63, 64, 68, 70, 87
    tyufyak cannon 31, 35, 70
Caspian Sea **9**, 81, 82
cavalry **18**, 25–26, **28**, **29**, 30, **31**, 32–35, 37 **38**, **39**, 41–42, **45**, 46, 53, 54, 55, 56, **62**, 64, 68, 78–79, 87
Chalem 79
chambuls 37, 41
Cheremis **12**, 45, 51, **61**, **66**, 85
    Meadow Cheremis 45, 52, 79
    Mountain Cheremis (Mari) 18–19, 34–35, 45, 79
Christianity 13, 19, 24, **35**, 38, 76, 78, **85**, 89, **91**
Chuvash 18, 52
Constantinople **38**, 85
Cossacks 13, 17, 34–35, 50, **52**, 55, 56, 84, 87, 89

Crimea 5, 10, 24, **43**, **44**, **47**, 75, 80, 84
Crimean Gate 7, **43**, **44**, 67
Crimean Khanate 5–6, **8**, **9**, 13, 19, 25, 35, **47**, **81**, 88
Crimeans 5, 10–11, 19, **20**, 21, 23, 39, 46, **48**, 50, 52, **61**, 84, **86**, 87

Donskoi, Grand Prince Dmitry **47**, 56, 70
drob 35, 64
dyeti boyarskiye 30, 32, 36, **56**, 74

Ediger-Magmet, Khan Prince 19, 21, 24–25, 41, 45, **50**, 52–54, 56, 65, 69, **71**, **74**, 76, **77**, 89
engineers 27, 31, 35–36, 53, 63

Galich **9**, 10, **24**
Giray, Khan Devlet 19, 20, 75, **86**, 87
Giray, Khan Safa 7, 10–11, 13, 21, 24, 89
Giray, Khan Saip 10–11, 13, 20
Giray, Utamish 13, 18, 89
Golden Horde **4**, 5, 40–41, **47**, 50, 65
Gorbaty-Shuisky, Prince Alexander 22–23, 26, **30**, 31, 46, 53, 55–56, **61**, **74**, 75, 77–78
guerrilla war 21, 26, 78–79
gulyai-gorod ('walking city') **61**, **61**, 84, **85**, **86**, 87
gunpowder **16**, 18, **28**, 33, 36, 45, 51, 63–65
Gury, Archbishop 79, 80

helmets 26, **29**, 32, **38**, 42, **68**, **69**, 85
Herberstein, Sigismund von **11**, 30

infantry 27–31, **32**, 33–35, 40, 42, **45**, 55–56, **57**, **61**, **74**, 78
Islam 13, 24, 42, **50**, 80, **85**, **89**, **91**
Ismail, Khan 79, 80, 84
Ivan III (Ivan the Great) **4**, 5, 7, **12**, 54, 63
Ivan IV (Ivan Vasilievich, *Grozny*, 'the Terrible') **4**, 6, **12**, 21, **22**, **24**, 28, **29**, 76, **81**, 83, **91**

Janissaries 19, **20**, 83, **85**, 87
Jenkinson, Anthony 32, 84

Kabat Gate **43**, 44, 65, **67**, 68
Kaluga 23, 48, **61**
Kashira 20, 46, 48
Kazan **4**, 5, **6**, 7, **8**, **9**, 10, **11**, **12**, 13, **16**, 17, **18**, **19**, 20, 21, 22–25, **26**, 27, **28**, 29, **30**, 33–37, **38**, 39–40, 41, **42**, **43**, **44**, **45**, 46–47, 48–49, 50, **51**, **52**, **53**, 54, **55**, 56, **57**, 60, **61**, **62**, 63, 65, **66–67**, 68–70, **71**, **74**, 75, 76, 77, 78, 79, 80, **81**, 85, 89–91, **92**
Kazan Chronicle **8**, 19, 27, 29, 68, 75
Kazan Khanate 5, **8**, **9**, **12**, 21, 35, 41, **81**
Khan's Gate **8**, **43**, 44, 67, 68, 70
Khan's Meadows **8**, **43**, 66
Khan's Palace **8**, **16**, **43**, 44, **66–67**, 68, 70, **74**, 88, 90
Khvorostinin, Prince Dmitry **86**, 87
Kolomna 5, 20, 21, 46, **48**, 52, **81**
kremlin **8**, 18, **20**, 84, 90
    Kazan Kremlin **6**, 25, 89
    Moscow Kremlin 18, 35, 63
Kuchum Khan **51**, 78
Kul Sharif Mosque **6**, **8**, 25, **26**, 70–71, 78, **89**, 90, **91**, **92**
Kulikovo **47**, 56
Kurbsky, Prince Andrei Mikhailovich **6**, 20, 22–23, **52**, **57**, 69, 75, 78
Kurlyatev-Obolensky, Dmitry 22–23

Lithuania 5, **9**, 11, 23, **25**, 54, **81**, 88
Livonian War 23–24, **81**, 87, 88

Mameshbirde 79
Massa, Isaac 38, 82–83
massacre 19, 23, 27
mestnichestvo 28, 29
Middle Volga region 85, 90
Mikulinsky, Prince Semyon 19, 21, 23, 25, 52, 79
mines 21, 36, 44, 62–63, 65, **66**
Mishätamaq 79
Mongols 37, **39**, **40**, **41**, **45**, 89
Mordvins **12**, 18, 35, 56
Moscow **4**, 5–6, 8, **9**, 10, **11**, 13, 17, **18**, 19, 20, 21, **24**, 25, 34, 35, 38, 45, **47**, **48**, **51**, 52, 54, 56–57, 63, 75, 76, 78, 79–80, **81**, 83–85, 87, 88–89, 91–92
Murom 10, **12**, 21, **47**, **48**, 54, 79
murzas 6, 25, 45, **53**, 68, 70, 87
Muscovite army 12, **16**, 17–19, 20, 21, 24, 29, 30, **32**, 33, 38–40, 52, 53–54, **55**, 56, **57**, 60, 61–62, 63, 64–65, **66–67**, 68–69, **74**, 75, 82–83, 85
Muscovy 4–5, **8**, **9**, 10, **11**, **12**, 20, 22, 24–25, 28–29, 33–35, 40, 46, 47, 50, 54, 70, 80, **81**, 87, 88

Nizhny Novgorod 9, 10, **12**, 13, 23, 46, 49, 54, 57, 79, **81**
Nogai 24, 41, **43**, 45, 50, **51**, 54, 70–71, 79, 80, 83–85, 87

Nogai Gate 43, 44, 65, 67
Nogai Khanate 6–7, 9, 12, 19, 24, 35, 44, 45, 75, 81
Nur Ali Gate 43, 44, 45, 67, 70

oghlans 6, 63, 74
Orthodox Church 80, 89–90, 91
Ottoman Empire 5, 8, 9, 10, 40, 80, 81, 85
Otuchev, Chapkyn 24–25, 68

pishchal 33, 34–35
Poland 9, 35, 81, 88
pomeshchiki 12–13, 18, 23, 30, 32, 34–35, 80
pososhnye lyudi 33, 36, 60, 64, 69
Pronsky-Shemyakin, Prince Yuri 31, 82–83
Pskov 9, 81, 90

Qasim Khanate 10, 19, 24, 34–35, 47

Razriadny Prikaz 24, 29
regiments (*polki*) 26, 27, 29–30, 34, 36, 41, 52, 68, 85
  Advance (*Peredovoi Polk*) 30, 47, 48, 53, 64–65, 67, 82, 86, 87
  Artillery 24, 31, 47, 48
  Guard (*Storozhevoi Polk*) 31, 47, 57, 67, 70, 87
  Left-Hand (*Lyevoi Ruki*) 23, 30–31, 44, 47, 48, 67, 68, 70
  Main (*Bolshoi*) 23, 30, 46–47, 48, 56, 64, 67, 68, 70, 87
  Right-Hand (*Pravoi Ruki*) 23, 30, 46–47, 48, 57, 63, 67, 70, 75, 86, 87
  Sentry 34, 47, 48
  Sovereign's 31, 47, 48, 67, 70–71
rivers:
  Bulak 7, 16, 42, 43, 44, 56, 62–63, 67, 70, 90

Kama 12, 49, 55–56, 79
Kazanka 6, 7, 8, 42, 43, 44, 53, 55, 62–63, 67, 70, 75, 79
Oka 11, 20, 38, 48
Shivoron 20, 50
Sura 47, 48–49
Sviyaga 17, 18
Volga 6, 9, 10, 12, 13, 17, 18, 19, 21, 23, 34, 45–47, 48–49, 50–52, 53, 54, 66, 75, 79–80, 81, 82–83, 84
Rossiyada 4, 22, 27, 40, 46, 52, 77, 89
Russia 4, 20, 33, 79, 89–90
Russification 78, 79, 80
Ryazan 5, 9, 20, 47, 48, 52

sabres 19, 30, 32, 34, 38, 40, 42
Selim I, Sultan 13, 37
Serebryany, Prince Pyotr 55–56
Serebryany-Obolensky, Prince Vasily 31, 46, 75, 77
Serebryany-Obolensky, Pyotr 17–18
service gentry 6, 12, 32, 80
Shabolat, Prince 25, 51, 54
Sharif, Kul 25, 71, 75
Shchenyatev, Pyotr 20, 30–31, 70
Shigalei, Khan 11, 18–19, 21, 24–25, 34, 47, 89
Shuisky, Prince Pyotr 30, 46, 53, 61, 79
Siberian Khanate 9, 50, 51, 78, 85
siege guns 13, 20, 33, 35, 46, 55, 60
siege tower 21, 60, 62–64, 66–67, 75
sotnik 30, 70
Söyembikä, Princess 13, 18, 89
Söyembikä Tower 89, 90
spears 18, 26, 28, 32–33, 42, 68
Streltsy 21, 31, 33, 34, 36, 55–57, 68, 74, 75, 84
Sviyazhsk 17, 18, 19, 21, 23–24, 45–47, 48–49, 52
Sylvester, Father 13, 22–23, 46

Tatars 4, 5, 6, 8, 10, 11, 17, 25, 26, 27, 30–31, 34–35, 37, 38, 39, 40, 41, 42, 45, 46, 47, 48, 50, 51, 52, 53, 54, 54, 55, 56–57, 61, 63–65, 68–71, 75, 78–80, 82, 84, 89, 90, 91
  Crimean Tartars 10, 19, 20, 37, 47, 52, 81, 83, 85–87
  Kazan Tatars 37–38, 90
  Mongol Tatars 5, 25, 31
Tatarstan 44, 50, 89, 91
Temnikov 35, 55
Tula 9, 19, 20, 21, 47, 48, 52, 81
Turnen Gate 43, 44, 65, 67

Udmurts 5, 12, 79
Uglich 17, 18
ulus 5, 45, 50
Ural Mountains 5, 50

Vasily III, Grand Duke 6, 10, 18, 24, 47, 54
Vladimir 12, 13, 47, 48
voivode (governor) 7, 10, 23, 30, 53, 70, 79, 82–83
Vorotynsky, Prince Mikhail 23, 30, 53, 64, 85, 86, 87
Vyazemsky, Alexander 82–83
Vyrodkov, Ivan Grigorievich 19, 23, 24, 31, 53, 60, 62–63, 66, 75

Water Gate 21, 43, 44, 63, 66–67

Yamghurchi, Khan 80, 82–84
Yapanchi, Prince 25–26, 51, 54–57, 66–67
Yertaul 30, 47, 53, 56, 65, 66

Zaynash 45, 70
Zboiviye Gate 43, 44, 64–65, 67